TALES FROM THE
KENTUCKY WILDCATS
LOCKER ROOM

TALES FROM THE
KENTUCKY WILDCATS
LOCKER ROOM

A COLLECTION OF THE GREATEST
WILDCAT STORIES EVER TOLD

DENNY TREASE
WITH RYAN CLARK

SPORTS
PUBLISHING

All interior photos courtesy of UK Sports Information Department

Sports Publishing books may be purchased in bulk at special discounts for sales promotion, corporate gifts, fund-raising, or educational purposes. Special editions can also be created to specifications. For details, contact the Special Sales Department, Sports Publishing, 307 West 36th Street, 11th Floor, New York, NY 10018 or sportspubbooks@skyhorsepublishing.com.

Sports Publishing® is a registered trademark of Skyhorse Publishing, Inc.®, a Delaware corporation.

Visit our website at www.sportspubbooks.com.

10 9 8 7 6 5 4 3 2

Library of Congress Cataloging-in-Publication Data is available on file.

ISBN: 978-1-61321-413-8

Printed in the United States of America

To my father,
who instilled in me an enduring
love for the game of basketball

Contents

ACKNOWLEDGMENTS

I could call this compilation of stories about Kentucky basketball a labor of love, but it wasn't a labor at all. It was a joy talking with so many of the players and coaches who helped to shape the university's remarkable basketball history.

Many of these stories have been told and retold for decades. Some no doubt have been embellished through the years. I merely attempted to confirm their original authenticity and to put them into a form that might link one to another. Some of the storytellers I contacted were more forthcoming than others. My old friend, Joe B. Hall, opened his home and his heart to me, talking long into the night about his most vivid memories, both as a player and a coach at Kentucky.

Former Wildcat Jerry Hale was most helpful in providing me with names and addresses of UK lettermen, nearly all of whom graciously gave me all the time I needed to pick their brains.

My thanks to UK basketball SID Brooks Downing for his help in finding pictures to go with many of the stories.

I make no claim that this book contains all of the best stories concerning basketball at the winningest college program in the land. My biggest challenge was deciding which ones deserved inclusion. At every turn, I attempted to find brand new stories, only to have someone down the road tell me, "Oh, yeah, I heard that one years ago."

Kentucky's rich basketball lore literally overflows with colorful anecdotes and touching remembrances. "Mr. Wildcat," Bill Keightley, was an eyewitness to many of the events that spurred these stories, and his willingness to rehash them with me provided enlightening insight.

My only hope is that as you read these stories, you will feel as energized as I did in compiling them.

I have saved the most heartfelt thank-you for my wife, Joyce, who read and reread each new entry in the book and encouraged me to keep going after I ran into the inevitable dead-ends. Her unfailing support and honest critiques have made the finished product better than it might have been.

FOREWORD
by
JOE B. HALL

One of the most enjoyable experiences a coach can have is to sit around with a group of his former players swapping old war stories. I'm not necessarily talking about specific games or wins and losses, but the inside stories about things the coach may not have even been aware of at the time. I've had many such experiences since my retirement from coaching, and *Tales from the Kentucky Wildcats Locker Room* provided me with many more without having to leave the comfort of my living room.

This is a collection of tales that people seldom see in newsprint but are exposed to only at group get-togethers where each shared memory leads to another. For me, this book brings back many wonderful memories of the players and coaches and supporters who meant so much to the University of Kentucky's rich basketball tradition. Denny Trease skillfully traces the glory years from the Rupp era all the way to the present as the tradition continues.

No one is better suited to compile these stories than Denny, whom I worked with through my first eight years as the head coach at Kentucky. Denny not only did the play-by-play of our games on television, but cohosted my weekly TV show. I remember he had a way of steering our conversation into areas that kept the program lively and entertaining and made it easy for me to communicate my message. He leads the reader through the pages of this book the same way.

I was not surprised when Denny fulfilled his boyhood dream of becoming a Major League Baseball announcer. He was a knowledgeable sportscaster who got that way with hard work, tireless preparation and an obvious love for what he did. It was also very obvious how much he appreciated the tradition associated with Kentucky basketball. I predict you will enjoy his easy, free-flowing style so much that you'll find it difficult to put the book down until every word has been digested.

Tales from the Kentucky Wildcats Locker Room is a fun read, but it's also a work of historical significance that brings out some of the strategy and facts never made public until now. And there's a tone to these stories sure to stir the emotions not only of devoted Cat fans, but of the casual reader as well. As the years go by, I'm sure all of us who love Kentucky basketball will take this book down off the shelf to reread and enjoy again and again.

—2002

TALES FROM THE
KENTUCKY WILDCATS
LOCKER ROOM

Adolph Rupp

PART ONE:

Adolph Rupp

A dolph Rupp became the basketball coach at the University of Kentucky in 1930. For forty-two years he patrolled the sidelines in his legendary brown suit and ended his career as the winningest coach in college basketball history. This son of German immigrants had a brilliant mind and a sharp wit that invariably left a lasting impression. Nearly all those who knew him have a favorite story about the "Baron of the Bluegrass."

• • •

LARRY CONLEY

Larry Conley is now a nationally respected basketball analyst on television. He was one of Rupp's all-time favorite players and a member of the 1966 NCAA runner-up squad known as Rupp's Runts, but Larry remembers getting off to a rough start with his famous coach.

Conley's high school career in Ashland, Kentucky, had produced 96 wins and only 9 losses, but on the first day of practice in his freshman year at UK, Larry was just

Larry Conley

weighing in at a scrawny 168 pounds when Coach Rupp strolled over to the scales and said, "Conley, you had a pretty good high school career. Who's the better coach, me or that feller who coached you up in Ashland?" Larry says he made the mistake of hesitating before giving his answer, and Rupp just shook his head in amazement and muttered, "Damn, son, you got a lot to learn."

By his senior season, Larry Conley had become a passing wizard known for his unselfish assists to leading scorers Pat Riley and Louie Dampier. Playing Indiana for the University of Kentucky Invitational Tournament championship that December, Conley actually scored the first 14 points of the game himself. Indiana called a timeout, and Conley remembers that as the Wildcats arrived back at their bench, Pat Riley put his arm around him and said, "All right, Larry, you got yours, now let us have ours." Conley didn't score another point the rest of the game.

Larry Conley is one of several former Wildcats who recall Rupp giving nearly the exact same speech every year on the first day of practice. Included in that speech was the now famous line: "Boys, we have a rule here. You don't speak unless you can improve the silence."

But for the sounds of rubber soles screeching on hardwood and an occasional bouncing ball (dribbling was always kept to a minimum during the Rupp regime), you could have heard a pin drop at Rupp's practice sessions.

• • •

TOM PARKER

Coach Rupp was more than willing to praise his players when they deserved it, although even the praise was often veiled in sarcasm. Tom Parker, a smooth southpaw forward who was named Southeastern Conference Player of the Year in Rupp's final season as Kentucky's coach, recalls a game against Indiana during his junior year. Hoosier star George McGinnis made a desperation shot from beyond midcourt that would have won the game for Indiana, but the officials ruled that an IU player had called timeout just prior to the shot. So the game went into overtime, and Parker combined with Larry Steele to score all of Kentucky's points in the extra session as the Wildcats won by a comfortable margin. The next day at practice, Coach Rupp walked in and said: "Boys, I want to introduce you to Mr. Parker and Mr. Steele. They didn't show up for the first 40 minutes against Indiana, but by-gawd, they sure showed up for the overtime."

• • •

SARCASM UNLIMITED

Once before a game in New York, the Wildcats were practicing at Madison Square Garden, where the court in those days had dead spots all over it. Seldom-used bench

Tom Parker

warmer Ernest Sparkman, from the tiny town of Carr Creek, Kentucky, was finding every one of those dead spots, dribbling the ball off his foot, dropping passes, and just generally making every mistake imaginable. Finally, Rupp stopped practice and said, "Ernest, would you please go over there in the corner and take a crap? I want you to be able to tell those good people in Carr Creek that you did something in Madison Square Garden."

• • •

UNBEATEN WITH NO PLACE TO GO

The 1953-54 Kentucky Wildcats were the only team in history to go undefeated and not win a national championship. In college basketball today, fifth-year seniors are celebrated, especially those who graduate in four years and take graduate classes while playing their final season. But after Kentucky went a perfect 25-0 during the 1953-54 regular season, star players Cliff Hagan, Frank Ramsey, and Lou Tsioropoulos were all declared ineligible for tournament play by the NCAA simply because they all had enough credits to graduate. Kentucky elected not to go to the tournament without them, and there are conflicting stories about how that decision came about. Some say the players voted 9 to 3 to go but Rupp vetoed their decision. Rupp himself insisted, "I would have taken them, yes sir, I really would have taken them and gone as far as we could have, but the athletic board voted not to go because without Hagan, Ramsey, and Tsioropoulos, they didn't think we had a chance. They thought we should let our record stand. That other story is absolutely wrong."

• • •

PETE GRIGSBY

Like most Kentucky recruits, Pete Grigsby was a high school basketball sensation, a 4-year starter for little Martin High School in southeastern Kentucky. Grigsby, who would go on to become a great high school coach in his own right, grew up listening to UK's Fabulous Five on the radio. He recalls, "It was my dream to play for the Wildcats, and when Adolph Rupp gave a speech at our high school athletics banquet, he signed me up that very night. All he had to do was wave his little finger at me, and I was ready to follow him back to Lexington."

Grigsby would play very little in his career at Kentucky. He was a victim of Coach Rupp's tendency to determine his top seven players and stick with them. "Seven might be stretching it. Some games it was more like his top six players," says Grigsby. "Many times through the years, I've wondered how different things might have been for me if Coach Rupp had used the same substitution patterns that so many coaches do today, going 10 or 11 deep on their bench."

Grigsby remembers several instances during the unbeaten 1953-54 season when the second five gave the starters all they could handle in practice. "Nobody could have could have come close to us if we'd gone to the NCAA tournament that year with Hagan, Ramsey, and Tsioropoulos, and even without them, I think we could have gone a long way. We had some really good players on the bench." Grigsby recalls the decision not to go to the tournament much differently than Rupp does. "He called each one of us into his office separately and said something like, 'Now you know we couldn't win without our three best players, so why ruin a perfect season by going up there and getting beat?' Then he called a team meeting and asked for a show of hands right out in the open. I think he phrased it something like, 'How many of you boys feel we should just stay home and let our record speak for itself rather than go up there and get our brains beat out?' Under those circumstances, not many were going to go against his wishes."

Pete Grigsby was an eyewitness to one of the most bizarre scenes in Kentucky basketball history. The Wildcats were playing St. Louis University at Kiel Auditorium in December of 1953. The arena was packed with St. Louis fans hoping Coach Ed Dickey and his Billikens could knock off the highly regarded Wildcats. Back then the timer at courtside often used a starter's pistol to signal the end of a half and to call teams back out onto the floor after a timeout. The timer that night was none other than Coach Dickey's son, Pat. In the second half,

Dickey fired the starter's pistol too close to Kentucky assistant coach Harry Lancaster on one end of the bench. Grigsby says he heard Lancaster warn Dickey never to do that again.

"Not long after that," says Grigsby, "the guy shot it off again just as close as before, and the next thing I see is Coach Lancaster grabbing the timer by the collar and punching him so hard he knocked him into the first row of seats. Ushers and security people came running down there and actually did a pretty good job of quieting things down. We eventually pulled out to 9- or 10-point lead, and the crowd started getting really worked up. About that time, Lou Tsioropoulos fouled out, and as he came back to the bench, the fans started getting on him, shouting some pretty nasty stuff, and he responded by giving them a one-finger salute. Women with high-heeled shoes came down behind our bench and started kicking us in the back and hitting us with their umbrellas. We hadn't done a thing, we weren't even playing, and yet we were getting whupped. I was never so glad for a game to end."

In the locker room after the game, Coach Rupp instructed the players to not even take showers and to just put their street clothes in their duffle bags, put their overcoats on over their warmups, and hustle out to some waiting taxicabs he had just called to the arena. "I don't know if he was worried the fans were gonna storm our locker room or what," says Grigsby, "but we did as he said, and I remember squeezing in beside the driver in the front of a taxi. Coach Rupp was in the back on the passenger side, and as we got about halfway back to the hotel, the taxi driver started talking about what a dirty team Kentucky was. I didn't know what was going to happen, but then Coach Rupp started agreeing with everything the guy was saying. Coach said, 'You're right, those Kentucky boys are mean as rattlesnakes. They shouldn't be allowed to play college basketball.' I'm sure the guy never had an inkling he was carrying some of those dirty Kentucky players and the coach that St. Louis fans loved to hate."

• • •

HARRY LANCASTER

Both Rupp and his longtime assistant, Harry Lancaster, were masters at using sarcasm to motivate players, and they would often provide simultaneous doses of it from opposite ends of the court. Lancaster, now deceased, described it as a "motivational crossfire." He once said: "Coach Rupp could ream a player until his asshole just hit the floor, and he had me doing it, too. I think the reason our players seldom buckled under the pressure of a game is that we put so much pressure on them during practice."

Back in the days when freshmen were ineligible to participate on the varsity level at Kentucky, Lancaster coached the first-year players through their own schedule, which included a number of junior college teams.

Several members of the 1954 UK freshman team recall a game against Sue Bennett Junior College. Kentucky scored at will against the outmanned juco players and built a 127-25 lead. When the dazed visitors from Sue Bennett called a timeout at that point, one of the Kentucky players asked Coach Lancaster what play they should run. Lancaster later admitted to being at a complete loss for words. "Frankly, I didn't know what to tell 'em," said Harry. "I had never been ahead by 102 points before."

• • •

TOMMY KRON

Even Tommy Kron, a hustler whose style of play was greatly admired by Rupp, felt the sting of the Baron's criticism during one particularly bad practice session. As Kron's misdeeds multiplied that day, Coach Rupp shook his head in disgust and muttered, "Son, I'm going to write a book some day on how not to play basketball, and I'm going to devote the first 200 pages to you." More than one player who came after Tommy Kron told me Rupp used the same line on them.

• • •

Pat Riley alongside Adolph Rupp

PAT RILEY

Pat Riley was another of Rupp's former players who went on to become an outstanding coach. Pat found his success in the NBA, playing with and coaching the Los Angeles Lakers, and later coaching the New York Knicks and the Miami Heat, but most Kentucky fans prefer to remember Riley from his playing days. He was a 6'3" forward with incredible leaping ability. In fact, Pat actually jumped center for "Rupp's Runts" in 1966, and in one remarkable stretch that season, he won the tip on 46 of 51 center jumps, many of them against players a half-foot taller. Riley later admitted, "Harry Lancaster taught me a little trick. As I went up, I'd plant my elbow in the other guy's shoulder, and he'd lift me up." Watch Riley's centers in the NBA and see how often they win the tip.

• • •

GAYLE ROSE

Gayle Rose, a talented guard on the Wildcats' unbeaten 1954 squad, says those grueling practice sessions under Rupp prepared him for all the challenges he's faced throughout his life. "Once I made it through some of the practices and Coach Rupp's biting criticism," says Rose, "nothing seemed too difficult anymore. I remember the year after I graduated, I was going through pilot training in Hondo, Texas, and the instructor was trying to solo me. I lost of couple of hundred feet my first time around so he had me try it again, and I lost another couple of hundred feet. He started really giving me what for, and I just started laughing. The fella asked me what was so funny, and I said, 'Sir, I've already been had by the master.'"

Rose has fond memories of the 1954-55 Kentucky team, of which little was expected after the departure of Cliff Hagan, Frank Ramsey, and Lou Tsioropoulos. Rose recalls, "We had a bunch of really scrappy players that season. The game I'll never forget was against Alabama at Memorial Coliseum. We were down at our end warming up before the game, and they were getting loose at the other end, and all of a sudden I noticed one of our reserve guards, Dan Chandler, jawing with this big 6'7" guy [Jim Bogan] from Alabama out near the midcourt stripe. Dan, who was only about 5'10", seemed to be taunting this guy, and the other fella was giving it back pretty good. Chandler, the son of former Kentucky Governor Happy Chandler, appeared to dare that big rascal to step across the line. Well, sure enough the guy stepped over, and the next thing you know, they were swinging at each other and pushing and shoving. I don't think any punches ever really landed, but finally they both went down in a heap. I was the closest player to 'em, and I thought, hey, I gotta break up this fight. So I grabbed the Alabama guy and just held on to him. The only problem was nobody grabbed Dan Chandler, and he jumped up and slugged the guy I had ahold of. Before I knew what was happening, one of the Alabama players got me a good lick right in the jaw, and players from both teams started going at it. When things finally quieted down, I remember thinking there was more tension in Memorial Coliseum than I had ever felt before. I think everybody was worried that the game itself might really get out of hand. But you know what? That turned out to be the cleanest game I ever played in. I guess everybody was on their best behavior, not wanting another fight to break out."

• • •

HERKY RUPP

Father coaching son has always been a bittersweet alliance. Many a coach in that situation has tried so hard not to show favoritism toward his own son that he ended up being harder on him than anyone else on the squad. Herky Rupp, who played for his famous father at Kentucky in the late fifties and early sixties, feels the two of them did a good job of separating their basketball relationship from the relationship they enjoyed at home. "If I needed to be chewed out," says Herky, "it seemed as though he would almost always have Coach Lancaster do it. Daddy had such great intelligence and wit that he was able to criticize players and officials during the course of a game without humiliating them just by injecting a little humor, but when he disciplined me at home, he left out the humor and got right to the point."

Herky recalls sharing more than one Christmas dinner with players who couldn't get home for the holidays. "That's a side of my father that rarely got publicized," says Herky, "and every year Daddy would buy up a big block of tickets to the Shrine Circus, take them over to the predominantly black neighborhood on Prall Street, and hand them out himself because he knew that was the only way most of those kids would ever get to see the circus."

When his grandson, Chip, was playing tee-ball at age 7, Adolph Rupp rarely missed a game. "Toward the end of the season," says Herky, "they decided to have a team picture taken, and they asked Daddy to be in it. He proudly posed for that picture, and later he personalized his autograph on each player's photo."

Anyone who witnessed Coach Rupp's tireless efforts on behalf of Shriners Hospital in Lexington knows that he had a soft spot in his heart for kids. That empathy was never more evident than with his own grandchildren. Herky Rupp remembers: "Daddy never liked to play cards. He thought it was a complete waste of time, but when Chip and Ferren were about six and four and for several years right in there, he would sit by the hour and play Go Fish, Old Maid, and Twenty-one. They used his footstool as a card table." The man who won 876 basketball games in his 42 years at Kentucky never won a single game of cards against his beloved grandkids.

• • •

BILLY THOMPSON

The late Billy Thompson covered the Wildcats for the *Lexington Herald-Leader* and hosted a weekly television show with Adolph Rupp for many years. Thompson probably had as much access to the Baron as anyone, although it should be noted that Rupp's phone number was listed in the Lexington telephone directory throughout his career.

Billy Thompson recalled phoning Rupp at his home on a Sunday evening just six days prior to the 1956-57 season opener. "I asked Uncle Adolph, 'If the season started tomorrow, who would your starting lineup be?' He thought about it for a moment and then rattled off five names, and I remember saying, 'Coach, you forgot a pretty fair country ball player in sophomore Johnny Cox.' Johnny had been a freshman sensation at UK after leading his Hazard High School team to the 1955 state championship. Adolph said, 'Johnny just hasn't been looking too good in practice.' I asked him if I could use that in a newspaper column for the next morning, and he said, 'Go right ahead.' So I did, and Coach Rupp later told me that he got a call that Monday afternoon from an irate fan in Hazard. Adolph said the phone was so hot that he dropped it, and when he picked it up, the caller told him that if Johnny Cox wasn't in the starting lineup for the opening game, there would be a hanging of a coach in Lexington, and it wouldn't be in effigy. Adolph said to me, 'You know, that darn boy started looking better that very afternoon.'"

• • •

HUMZEY YESSIN

Humzey Yessin served as team manager under Rupp during the glorious era from 1946 through '49 and later served as scout and finally confidante to Rupp right up until the Baron's death in 1977. Yessin saw both the tough and the tender sides of Adolph Rupp on many occasions. Humzey's ancestors had come from Syria, but Rupp had trouble recalling that fact and always referred to Yessin as "the little Armenian."

Prior to the inaugural University of Kentucky Invitational Tournament in 1955, Yessin along with Buddy Parker and Baldy Gilb had scouted the Wildcats' opponent in the finals, the top-ranked Dayton Flyers, and the three of them were seated right behind the Kentucky bench when the game against Dayton began. Dayton opened up a 12-point lead in the first half, and Rupp suddenly turned to the trio behind him and asked, "Have you fellers got any ideas to help us get this thing turned around?" Humzey now says, "We just kind of looked at each other, and finally Buddy Parker piped up, 'If we pick 'em up all over the court, I think we can force some turnovers.' Baldy and I shook our heads like we agreed, and Coach Rupp promptly switched to a full-court pressure defense. Unfortunately Dayton was ready for it. They brought their All-American center, Bill Uhl, out to midcourt to help out and as they cut off of him, he made crisp passes that just carved up the Kentucky defense. Dayton's lead suddenly went from 12 to 20 points. Adolph called timeout, turned to the three of us and said, 'I hope you fellers don't have any more bright ideas.'"

The next morning, Yessin got a call from Coach Rupp, who demanded that Humzey come see him immediately. Yessin fretted all the way there that Rupp was going to blame him for the loss. Instead, Coach Rupp greeted him warmly and presented Yessin with a tournament wristwatch, saying, "I had hoped you would come to the tournament banquet so I could give you this. You've done a lot for our program. In fact, you're my favorite little Armenian." Rupp's comments were seldom as kind around his players.

• • •

DICKY PARSONS

As sharp as Rupp was at devising strategy to take advantage of the opponent's weaknesses, he often had trouble remembering the names of his own players. Dicky Parsons, a hustling guard from Harlan, Kentucky, played three seasons under Rupp, beginning with the 1958-59 campaign. Parsons says, "Throughout my career, Coach Rupp called me Bobby about as much as he called me Dicky. At first, I was hurt to think that he didn't know my name, but when I finally realized that I reminded him of Bobby Watson, one of the stars of the 1951 national championship team, I considered it an honor that he thought of me in the same terms as Bobby Watson."

Parsons was one of three new guards fighting for playing time in his sophomore season. Bennie Coffman and Sid Cohen had just come from the junior college ranks, and the three of them were doing their best in practice to show Coach Rupp that they could score. "One day Rupp stopped practice," says Parsons. "He walked up to our star forward, Johnny Cox, and said, 'You were an All-American last year, weren't you, Johnny?' Cox, who never said much, just mumbled, 'Yessir,' and Coach replied, 'Well, I'm sorry to have to inform you that you won't be an All-American this year because we don't have any guards smart enough to pass you the ball.'" Dicky Parsons says, "That was just Coach Rupp's subtle way of reminding us to concentrate more on playmaking and less on scoring."

• • •

READ MORGAN

Rupp's Wildcats were playing DePaul in Chicago in 1949. At practice the day before the game, it was bitterly cold inside Chicago Stadium because the court had been put down right over the ice for a Blackhawks hockey game that night. In those days, it was legal for college teams to work out players who wanted to transfer from another school. Read Morgan was such a player. He had contacted Coach Rupp about wanting to transfer from Wisconsin to UK, and his workout that morning in Chicago was nothing short of sensational. Despite the frigid temperature inside the building, Morgan made practically every shot he took, and afterwards Coach Rupp told anyone who would listen, "Keep an eye on this boy, Read Morgan. I believe the Boston Celtics just turned him loose, and he's going to become a great player for us."

Rupp often predicted a player's future based on the way that player ate. He preferred players who wolfed down each bite as if it might be their last. Watching Read Morgan eat at a small, family-style restaurant in New York the next year, Rupp again predicted greatness. "By-gawd, the boy eats with determination," said Rupp. "He grabbed that plate right out of the waitress's hand and gobbled up everything on it before she even got back to the kitchen." Rupp then went into a comparison between Morgan and a seldom-used player named Johnny Stough, an Alabama native with genteel, southern manners. "Johnny Stough cuts a nice little piece of steak, then puts his knife down, switches the fork to his right hand, takes a bite, chews it ever so slowly, and then dabs his mouth with his napkin before cutting another little piece. But he plays basketball the same way, with no aggressiveness. This boy Morgan over here attacks his meat with a vengeance."

Rupp's prediction of basketball greatness for Read Morgan never came true. Morgan enrolled in a drama class at UK, let his short, marine-style haircut grow out into long ducktails and suddenly couldn't do anything right on the basketball court. As the talented transfer became more and more interested in acting, Coach Rupp decided to "fire him" from the basketball team, but being a pussycat at heart, Rupp ordered his assistant, Harry Lancaster, to carry out the firing. Morgan couldn't believe what he was hearing from Lancaster, so he went straight to Rupp to see if it was really true. Rupp sadly shook his head and said, "I'm afraid so, son. The next time you see me, you'll have to buy a ticket to do it." Read Morgan, by the way, became a successful actor and appeared on the popular TV series *Playhouse 90.*

• • •

CLIFF HAGAN

In 1953, no player in Southeastern Conference history had ever scored more than 50 points in a game, but perhaps no SEC player to that point had the combined grace and athleticism of Kentucky's Cliff Hagan. A somewhat undersized forward at 6'4", Hagan had developed an unstoppable hook shot as a high school player in Owensboro.

On December 5, 1953, in a game against Temple, Hagan started hitting that hook shot from every angle and piling up points at a remarkable rate. With 43 seconds left in the game, Cliff scored his 50th and 51st points

Cliff Hagan

to break the conference scoring record of his future NBA teammate, Bob Pettit.

Looking back on that game, Adolph Rupp once said, "I was going to break him of that hook shot, but every time I got ready to make him stop using the thing, he would hit four or five in a row, and I'd say to myself, 'I'll break him next week.'"

• • •

BILLY RAY LICKERT

Billy Ray Lickert was a sharpshooting guard who helped Kentucky win what Adolph Rupp often described as one of the best games ever played at Memorial Coliseum. The mighty Ohio State Buckeyes, with future NBA greats Jerry Lucas and John Havlicek, were in town for a December game in 1959. With Lucas leading the way, Ohio State raced to a 59-49 halftime lead.

Lickert recalls that all Coach Rupp wanted to talk about in the locker room during the break was the fact that no Kentucky team had ever given up a hundred points on its home court. Rupp told them, "It sure looks like you boys are gonna become the first team to do such a thing." Lickert says, "We all thought at the time that the old SOB had given up on us and the only thing he cared about was holding down the final score, but looking back on it through the years, I can see that was just

Billy Ray Lickert

his way of motivating us. Coach Rupp knew that if we held them under a hundred, it would mean Ohio State could only score 41 points in the second half, and we had already poured in more than that."

Kentucky came out in the second half running the old Auburn shuffle offense that freed up Lickert and his backcourt mate Bennie Coffman for one open shot after another, and they seldom missed. Lickert and Coffman combined for 55 points that night as Kentucky stormed from behind to win 96-93.

Billy Ray Lickert was a small boy of nine or ten when he first met Adolph Rupp, and it was an encounter he has never forgotten. Coach Rupp had written a book entitled *Rupp's Championship Basketball*, and Billy Ray took his copy to get it autographed by the legendary coach at one of the Wildcats' public scrimmages at the old Alumni Gym.

With Rupp standing idly by watching his players warm up that night, young Lickert decided the time was right to go after his autograph, but as Billy Ray approached his target, a ball came bouncing right in his direction. The never-bashful Billy Ray just grabbed it and launched a shot that hit the side of the backboard and bounced right back to him. Lickert fired up a second shot as Coach Rupp noticed what was going on and barked, "Boy, get out of this gym right this minute." Billy Ray, who went on to become Kentucky's Mr. Basketball after a great career at Lafayette High School in Lexington, eventually got Rupp's autograph, but more importantly, Coach Rupp got Lickert's signature on a scholarship to the University of Kentucky.

• • •

BILL SPIVEY

As a teenager in Warner Robbins, Georgia, Bill Spivey was definitely too big for his own good. He actually played a year of high school ball without shoes. The school didn't have any big enough to fit him, so Spivey played in three pairs of sweat socks and slid every time he tried to make a move.

Adolph Rupp never tired of telling the story of how he corralled his first seven-footer. "I was intrigued when Spivey came in here and said he wanted to play for us," Rupp recounted. "But oh, he was a mess. He was seven feet tall and only weighed 160 or 165 pounds. We decided to take a chance on him, and I said, 'Bill, if you can gain 40 pounds, you can play here. If you can't, you won't.' He said, 'I think I can. If I eat regularly and get plenty, I'll make it, Coach.'"

"Well, we got him here that summer and he got a job at Owen Williams's drug store," said Rupp. "Bill could reach up and clean those fluorescent lights without needing a ladder. Harry [Lancaster] made him drink four malted milks a day with eggs in them, and Bill started putting on the weight. I was in England. That was the year of the Olympics, and I finally got a letter from Harry who said that Bill now weighed 200 pounds, so I cabled him back collect and said, 'I'm convinced he can eat, but can he play basketball?'"

The answer to that question proved to be a definitive yes. Spivey averaged just over 19 points per game in both

Bill Spivey

his sophomore and junior years and led Kentucky to its third NCAA Championship in 1951.

• • •

JOCK SUTHERLAND

Rupp demanded respect from his players and fellow coaches, but he gave it grudgingly. Jock Sutherland was one of the outstanding high school coaches in the state of Kentucky when Assistant Coach Lancaster hired him to scout the Wildcats' next opponent, Vanderbilt, in Nashville. Sutherland would later be a part of C. M. Newton's coaching staff at Alabama before returning to the high school ranks to win a state championship at Lexington Lafayette. He recalls staying up until the wee hours of the morning to type his thick scouting report on Vanderbilt and then jumping in the car after just two hours of sleep to make the long drive to Lexington. Jock was admittedly nervous when he finally arrived at the UK campus and hustled into Memorial Coliseum, where he literally ran into Coach Rupp in the hallway.

Sutherland remembers their encounter this way: "As a young boy growing up in Lexington, I had idolized Coach Rupp, and I almost bowed at his feet as I handed him my stack of paperwork and stammered, 'Here's your scouting report on Vanderbilt.' He looked at me like I was an alien that had just dropped out of the sky and said, 'Scouting report? This looks more like Webster's Dictionary.' With that, he threw the report into a trash can, turned back to me and roared, 'Just tell me what we have to do to beat 'em!'"

Sutherland was told to be on the practice floor that afternoon to help walk the players through the game plan, and when he arrived, Rupp introduced him by saying, "Harry's friend here is gonna give you boys some pointers on how to stop Vanderbilt." When Jock finished his remarks, Coach Rupp turned to his assistant and said, "Harry, you can take your friend out of here now." Sutherland wasn't even allowed to watch the rest of the practice.

• • •

LOUIE DAMPIER

Louie Dampier scored 1,575 points in his career at Kentucky, the tenth highest total in school history. But the little guard from Indianapolis can only wonder how many more he could have added to that total if the 3-point shot had been in effect in the late sixties. Adolph Rupp once said, "Dampier was the greatest outside shooter I ever saw. God taught him how to shoot, and I took credit for it."

• • •

THE RECRUITING TRAIL

Tact was never Rupp's strong point, and his assistants often had to smooth over hurt feelings. Joe B. Hall, who would eventually succeed Rupp as head coach, remembers a recruiting trip to Indiana for which the plan was to see two high school stars in different gyms on the same night. The first stop was Marion, Indiana, where Greg Starrick was the local phenom. Rupp and Hall were scheduled to watch the first quarter of that game, drive to Benton, Indiana, to catch the end of a game featuring future Georgia Tech star Rich Younkas, and then drive back to Marion for a postgame meeting with the Starrick family. Rupp and Hall were given seats in the stands right next to Greg Starrick's grandmother, and not long after tipoff, Coach Rupp grumbled, loud enough for everyone within six rows to hear, "Joe, I forgot my glasses. Which one is the little bastard?"

Under the circumstances, Hall remembers being only too glad to escape Grandma's glare and head for Benton after a quarter in which Starrick had missed every shot he'd taken. Upon their return to Marion later that evening, Hall asked Greg Starrick how the game had come out. The reply was a terse, "We won in overtime." Joe B. kept the conversation going by asking, "Did you have a good game?" Starrick answered, "Yes, sir, pretty good." Eager to find out if the youngster had ever regained his shooting eye that night, Hall asked how many points Starrick had scored. The answer will remain etched in the memory of Joe B. Hall forever.

"86."

Greg Starrick had scored a record 86 points that night, and the two Kentucky coaches had not seen a single one of them.

• • •

DAN ISSEL

Dan Issel is Kentucky's all-time leading scorer, having poured in 2,138 points in three seasons from 1967 to 1970, but interestingly enough, Dan was not UK's first choice among the big men they were recruiting during his senior year of high school. In fact, when Issel made his official visit to the Kentucky campus, he happened to read a newspaper article about Kentucky's recruiting prospects and was surprised to find that his name wasn't even mentioned.

Joe B. Hall, Kentucky's primary recruiter at that time, says, "Even though a couple of other centers we were after may have had glossier reputations, Issel was a player with great potential, and we didn't want to let him get away."

Dan did manage to get away, at least for a few hours, on the night Hall made his in-house visit to Batavia, Illinois. Issel told Hall that he had a date that night and would only be able to spend an hour with him. Hall assured him an hour would be sufficient, and sure enough,

Dan Issel

Dan hauled his 6'8" frame right out the door after an hour of conversation. Joe Hall stayed on to continue his sales pitch to Dan's mother and dad.

Mr. Issel went off to bed at 10 o'clock as he always did, but Hall still didn't get up to leave. Dan Issel, the future ABA and NBA All-Star, says, "When I walked back into the house about 11 o'clock, Coach Hall was still sitting there giving his recruiting pitch to my mom, and I guess it worked."

There is one game in Issel's illustrious career that he would love to play over again. His Wildcats were ranked No. 1 in the country when they took on Jacksonville in the 1970 Mideast Regional Finals in Columbus, Ohio. Issel led all scorers in that game with 28 points, despite fouling out with 10:16 left to play. Big Dan picked up his fifth foul as he was running back down the court after a Jacksonville basket. He simply looked back over his shoulder to see if the guards needed any help bringing the ball up, and at that instant, Jacksonville's 5'10" point guard, Vaughn Wedeking, ran up and stopped directly in front of Issel. Dan ran right over him, and when the official's whistle blew, Issel knew he would never add another point to his record total at Kentucky.

Jacksonville won the game 106 to 100. Adolph Rupp later called it perhaps the most disappointing loss of his career, partly because it deprived Dan Issel of his last chance to appear in the Final Four.

• • •

JERRY HALE

Rupp hated losing, no matter who the opponent happened to be. In 1971, the Kentucky freshman team included seven highly sought-after recruits who had been dubbed "the Super Kittens." Jerry Hale, a hustling guard on that talented but baby-faced unit, remembers losing their first scrimmage against the varsity that season by 53 points. But the Super Kittens gained confidence as the year progressed, and one day they found themselves leading the varsity at the end of practice. Rupp was famous for his short, crisp practice sessions that almost never extended beyond the prescribed hour and a half, but after two grueling hours on that particular day, he ordered the players to just keep scrimmaging. Not until the varsity finally regained the lead did Rupp walk to center court and proclaim, "Good practice, boys, now hit the showers."

Jerry Hale, meanwhile, is the subject of one of the most inspiring stories in Kentucky basketball lore. On March 7, 1966, Jerry was a 12-year-old Wildcat fan attending a game at Memorial Coliseum with his father. Rupp's Runts had just been voted the No. 1 team in the country, and to celebrate the occasion, the famous UK basketball booster club, the Committee of 101, wheeled a huge six-foot-high cake out onto the court. When Coach Rupp got on the PA system and invited the fans to come down from their seats to get a piece of the cake, little Jerry Hale was one of the first to take him up on the offer. But while others in the crowd were happily devouring their cake, Jerry wrapped his in a napkin and kept it on his lap during the long drive home to New Albany, Indiana. When his dad finally asked, "Aren't you going to eat your cake?" Jerry answered, "No, not until the day I sign a scholarship to play basketball at the University of Kentucky."

Five years later, after endless hours of practicing his basketball skills, Jerry Hale, by then the star player at Floyd Central High School, was the guest of honor at a school assembly at which he officially accepted a scholarship offer from the most successful college basketball program in the land. The small piece of cake was removed from the freezer, and Jerry started to take a bite in celebration. But before that sweet icing ever reached his lips, Hale stopped and said, "No, I'm not going to eat this until my team wins another national championship for the University of Kentucky."

When the Cats went to the Final Four in San Diego in Jerry's senior year, his parents packed the cake in dry ice and took it with them. Kentucky endured a narrow loss to UCLA in the championship game. Jerry Hale had come within one victory of fulfilling a double-layered dream.

• • •

JIM ANDREWS

Jim Andrews, a dominating 6'11" center who played under both Rupp and Joe B. Hall, remembers that the Baron treated every victory the same, no matter how big the margin. According to Andrews, Rupp's opening locker room comments never varied after a win, whether he had just witnessed a fifty-point trouncing or a nail-biting, one-point squeaker. The winningest coach on the planet at the time would always say, "I want to thank you boys for adding another win to our total." Then he might spend the next ten minutes pointing out the mistakes within that victory, but his opening sentiment was in keeping with the line so often credited to Rupp, "If it matters not whether you win or lose, what's that scoreboard up there for?"

• • •

THE WAR DEPARTMENT

Mike McKenzie covered Southeastern Conference basketball in the 1970s for newspapers in Huntsville and Tuscaloosa, Alabama; Atlanta Georgia; and Baton Rouge, Louisiana. He recalls interviewing Rupp in his motel room the night before a game in Auburn, Alabama. "We were having a delightful conversation when Coach Rupp suddenly got up and said, 'We'll continue this in a little while, just make yourself at home, but I've found that whenever I'm on the road about this time of night, I have to check in with the War Department, so if you'll excuse me now.' Adolph then spent the next half hour or so on the phone discussing family matters with his wife before completing our interview."

• • •

WAH WAH JONES

Wah Wah Jones has often been described as the most talented all-around athlete ever to play at Kentucky. To earn such praise, Jones won four varsity letters in football, four in basketball and three in baseball. He would have won a fourth letter as a pitcher and first baseman on the diamond, but following his senior season of basketball, Jones and other members of the two-time national champion Fabulous Five turned pro and conducted a lucrative barnstorming tour around the country.

Wah Wah got his colorful nickname as a small boy simply because his little sister, Jackie, some three years younger, couldn't pronounce his given name, Wallace. In basketball, Wah Wah Jones set a national high school scoring record in the small Eastern Kentucky town of Harlan.

He cracked the starting lineup as a freshman at Kentucky and was the second leading scorer on the 1946 team that went 28-2 and won the NIT, which then carried equal status with the NCAA tournament.

Wah Wah's older brother Hugh played for the University of Tennessee, and on one memorable road trip to Knoxville, Coach Rupp was ranting and raving to the players about the setting. Jones remembers the occasion like this: "Rupp told us that the sun never shines in Knoxville. He said, 'Everybody in this God-forsaken place is a no-account sum bitch.' But then he noticed me sitting over in the corner and he said, 'Everybody, Wah Wah, except your brother Hugh. He's a fine young man who served his country in the army. I just wish he had come back and played for us at Kentucky.'"

Jones wanted to give up football and concentrate solely on basketball in his sophomore year, but the Wildcats' new football coach, Paul "Bear" Bryant, would have none of that idea. Jones says, "Coach Bryant was a tough customer and very persuasive. He wasn't about to let Coach Rupp have the exclusive use of my services."

The next year, Wah Wah injured his ankle toward the end of the football season and was late reporting for basketball practice. "Rupp was always using football against me," says Jones. "Even after I was completely healthy again, he was slow to play me, claiming I wasn't in good basketball shape.

"About seven or eight games into that 1947-48 season," recalls Jones, "we made an eastern road trip to play Temple in Philadelphia and St. John's in New York. On the road, Coach Rupp would retire to his hotel room,

Wah Wah Jones

put on his red pajamas, and then summon a writer or a coach or an athletic director to come up and socialize with him. After Temple beat us, Adolph ordered team manager Humzey Yessin, my old high school teammate from Harlan, to come up and talk with him. Coach asked Humzey what he thought was wrong with the Wildcats, and Yessin told him, 'We'll start playing better when you get Wah Wah back in the starting lineup.'

"Well, Rupp accused Humzey of not being objective and showing favoritism toward his old friend from Harlan, but I started the next night against St. John's and scored 16 points as we won impressively. He kept me in there the rest of the season, and we finished 36-3 and won the NCAA championship."

Jones and his Kentucky teammates from the Fabulous Five, Alex Groza, Ralph Beard, Kenny Rollins, and Cliff Barker, went on to the 1948 Olympics and helped the U.S. win the gold medal despite what Wah Wah called the worst officiating he had ever seen. "The refs didn't speak English," says Jones, "and we had no idea what they were saying or why they were making so many strange calls."

The following year, Kentucky added its second consecutive NCAA title, and Wah Wah Jones added boxing to his considerable athletic skills. Jones fouled out of a game in Boston against Holy Cross, and as he returned to the bench, he had words with a fan who had been heckling him throughout the game. Wah Wah says, "The guy threw his program at me." Other witnesses say it was a wadded-up paper cup, but there is no disputing what happened next. Jones grabbed the man and slugged him so hard that the buttons on his shirt popped. Assistant coach Harry Lancaster had to help Wah Wah fight his way out of the mass of irate Holy Cross fans.

• • •

RALPH BEARD

Adolph Rupp once said, "Ralph Beard is the greatest basketball player I ever saw." Beard, a 5'10" guard from Louisville, graced the first-ever cover of *Sports Illustrated.* In his four years at Kentucky, Ralph never lost a game in conference play. The teams on which he played went a perfect 55-0 against SEC competition. Perhaps even more remarkable was their average margin of victory, a whopping 28 points per game.

Like many boys growing up in Kentucky, Ralph Beard was indoctrinated into the game of basketball at a very young age. His mother, Sue Beard, told the story of Ralph's earliest exposure to the game. "His first basket was his potty chair," said Sue. "He'd throw a little rubber ball at the chair. As he got older, he used the cutaway part of his high chair. Then we put a miniature basket over his bed. Then we tacked it up on the kitchen door. Finally, we had to move it outside in the yard."

Ralph Beard's shooting prowess was developed through many years of practice, but his speed came naturally. That speed was summed up in Adolph Rupp's vivid description: "When Beard ran, you could smell the rubber burning."

• • •

THE COWBOY

Leroy "Cowboy" Edwards was Kentucky's first great center, although Rupp and Wildcat fans only got to enjoy his talents for one season. Edwards, a 6'5" muscleman once described by Rupp as "the strongest player on earth," single-handedly outscored Kentucky's first five opponents in the 1934-35 campaign. His 343 points in 21 games that season were more than any UK player before him. Edwards, though, abruptly accepted an offer of $2,400 to leave the Wildcats and play for a semipro team in Indianapolis. Rupp's annual salary was only $2,800 at the time, so he wasn't totally surprised by Edwards' decision.

Decades later, after Kentucky lost to 7'2" Artis Gilmore and his Jacksonville University team in the 1970 NCAA Tournament, newspaper reporters asked Rupp if Gilmore was the best pivot man he had ever seen. Rupp answered simply, "No. Edwards was better." The reporters had absolutely no idea who he was talking about.

JOHN CRIGLER

John Crigler was a rugged forward on the 1958 national championship team that came to be known as "The Fiddlin' Five." Crigler remembers playing the worst game of his career in the national semifinals that year against Temple. "I just couldn't buy a basket that night, and I think that's why Seattle decided to have their star player, Elgin Baylor, guard me in the championship game," said Crigler. "They figured he wouldn't have to expend much energy and wouldn't get in foul trouble just staying with me. But Coach Rupp had gotten a midnight phone call the night before from a coach out west who had played against Seattle. The coach suggested the only way to beat them was to take the ball right at Elgin Baylor. Rupp knew I had confidence in my ability to drive in and get a shot off against just about anybody, and that was our game plan against Seattle. I kept driving to the basket and scoring, and before you knew it, Elgin Baylor had picked up his third foul."

Seattle eventually had to go to a zone to protect Baylor, and when they did, Johnny Cox started hitting from outside and Vern Hatton just scored from everywhere. Hatton finished with a game-high 30 points, but the 14 scored by Crigler may have been the key to Kentucky's 84-72 win.

• • •

TERRY MOBLEY

Kentucky vs. Duke is considered one of the great rivalries in college basketball today, but Terry Mobley, who became UK's interim athletics director in early 2002, can attest to the fact that the rivalry didn't begin with the NCAA championship game in 1978.

When the Wildcats and the Blue Devils squared off in the finals of the 1963 Sugar Bowl Tournament in New Orleans, the game featured a great individual matchup. Kentucky's Cotton Nash and Duke's Jeff Mullins were two of the premier players in the country that season, and the matchup took on added significance because Mullins had been a high school star at Lexington's Lafayette High School, almost within shouting distance of the University of Kentucky.

The 1963 contest see-sawed back and forth with neither team able to build a substantial advantage. Terry Mobley's jumper tied the game at 79 with less than a half minute to play, and the remainder of the game is still fresh in his mind all these years later. "Tommy Kron was just starting to build his reputation as a defensive pickpocket," says Mobley, "and Coach Rupp had put Tommy in for Randy Embry. That move really paid off when Tommy managed to steal the ball, allowing us to call time out with seven seconds left."

Everybody in the arena that night, including Mobley, knew that Cotton Nash would be called upon to take the potential game-winning shot. Terry recalls, "Cotton hadn't done squat in the first half, but he came back and had a great second half, so when we put the ball in play, none of us were too surprised that Duke sagged back in around Nash, covering him like a blanket. I found myself open with four or five seconds to go, and I really had no choice but to shoot it."

The shot went in, and with Duke having already used all its timeouts, the Kentucky celebration began. As Mobley received congratulatory hugs and handshakes in the wild scene at center court, he noticed a strange sight out of the corner of his eye. "Coach Rupp never came out onto the court to congratulate us after a win," says Mobley, "but this time I noticed him hurrying straight toward me. He always called me by the name of my hometown, and this time he got close enough that I couldn't mistake his words, and he said, 'Remember, Harrodsburg, we knew Duke was expecting Nash to get the ball, so we outsmarted them and instructed you to take the last shot.'"

When Mobley picked up a New Orleans newspaper the next morning, he couldn't help laughing when he read the headline: RUPP SURPRISES DUKE—CALLS ON MOBLEY TO TAKE THE WINNING SHOT.

Terry Mobley says Adolph Rupp was one of the funniest people he ever ran across. "Coach could tickle a dead man," says Mobley. "I remember a practice my junior year when we were working on an inbounds play under our own basket to try to get a quick score. Coach said, 'Now, Harrodsburg, before you make your break to the ball from the other side, just kinda act nonchalant, pretend to be disinterested, act stupid. Aw, hell, just act natural, and the play is bound to work.' We always tried not to laugh, but it wasn't easy."

• • •

ED BECK

Ed Beck was a rebounding and defensive specialist on the 1958 NCAA championship squad. He had a strong religious faith when he arrived on the Kentucky campus and later became a Methodist minister. He needed all the faith he could muster when his wife, Billie, died of cancer in the spring of Ed's junior year. That ordeal enabled Beck to see Adolph Rupp in a much different light than many of the other players before and after him.

Billie Beck was a slim, 5'6", bronze-skinned beauty with a well-developed sense of humor and a devotion to caring for others through her job as a nurse. Her cancer had already been diagnosed when she agreed to marry Ed Beck only under the condition that he promise never to leave the University of Kentucky because of her illness.

Barely a week after their wedding, Ed was scheduled to begin his sophomore year of classes at UK. Billie was to undergo another round of cancer treatments in Georgia before joining Ed to set up housekeeping in Lexington. However, at the last minute, Billie convinced her doctors to postpone the treatments just long enough for her to spend the first week of school in Kentucky with Ed. When the newlyweds dropped into Memorial Coliseum to meet Coach Rupp, he insisted that Ed go do whatever he needed to do to get his class schedule worked out and that the coaches would take good care of Billie. Rupp took an instant liking to this pretty southern belle and spent the entire morning learning more about her and delighting Billie with his storytelling.

Ed says, "Throughout Billie's illness, Coach Rupp sent her flowers, wrote her letters, called her and just did everything he could to keep her spirits up. We lost to Michigan State in the Midwest Regional championship game that year after leading most of the way, and just before entering the locker room afterwards, I walked up to Coach Lancaster to apologize for how badly we had played in the closing moments of the game. I told him I just didn't understand how we let it slip away, and I'll never forget his reply to me. He said, 'Some day, we'll know the reason why.' I think we found out the reason when my wife died the following Saturday. If we had beaten Michigan State, we would have been in Kansas City playing for the national championship that day. Coach Rupp was there in Kansas City as a spectator when he got word that Billie had died. He immediately caught a plane to Georgia to be with me and attend the funeral the next day."

The following night, Coach Rupp got up at the team banquet back in Lexington and gave a moving speech about how Billie "showed us all what strength, determination, and commitment are all about." He dedicated the following season to her memory.

On the one-year anniversary of Billie Beck's death, Kentucky beat Seattle for the 1958 NCAA championship.

With Ed Beck's preaching background, it's no wonder that one of his most vivid memories is of the night that Vernon Hatton's 47-foot prayer was answered at Memorial Coliseum. Beck recalls, "We were trailing Temple by two points with only one second left in overtime, and Coach Rupp called time out and diagrammed an inbounds play to get the ball to Vernon. Coach told him, 'Get your feet set pointing right toward the basket so when you catch the pass, you can shoot without having to turn anything but your upper body.' Temple fell back to guard against a long pass underneath. I was stationed right in front of the basket, and as that shot sailed toward me, I could see it was dead-on perfect all the way. It went in with a swish to send the game into a second overtime, and people who had already left the Coliseum came back in from the parking lots to watch us win the game in three overtimes." Perhaps Billie Beck was guiding that shot from above.

• • •

VERNON HATTON

The day after Hatton's miraculous heave against Temple, he walked into Coach Rupp's office and politely asked if there was any chance he could have the game ball as a keepsake. Rupp reacted with total indignation, going on and on about how upset the UK Athletic Department would be if he gave away a $35 basketball. Just when Vern Hatton had gotten almost angry enough to strangle his coach, Rupp cracked a smile, pulled the basketball out from under his desk, flipped it to Hatton and congratulated him for his clutch performance.

• • •

FAREWELL BARON

In the summer of 1977, I was sports director of the local CBS television affiliate in Lexington, and Coach Rupp was in failing health. I was planning an hour-long documentary entitled *Farewell Baron* that would not be aired until Rupp's death. With that in mind I arranged an in-depth, wide-ranging interview to be done in his home.

I made no attempt to cover up the purpose of our *This Is Your Life*-style interview. We both knew when and how that footage would be used. After what seemed like hours of give and take, I asked my final question. "If you could write your own epitaph, sir, what words would you put there on you tombstone?" Knowing his mastery of the language and his flare for the dramatic, I was surprised by the simplicity of his answer. As tears formed in his eyes, Adolph Rupp quietly summed up his career and his life like this: "I would say he was a man who always did the best he could."

Rupp died on December 11, 1977, as his beloved Wildcats were playing the University of Kansas in Lawrence, where Rupp himself had played his college basketball under the great Phog Allen.

In every one of his life's endeavors, Adolph had been a meticulous planner, and so it came as no shock when former Kentucky Governor A. B. "Happy" Chandler later told me that Rupp had even selected his pallbearers far in advance, saying he wanted "men with enthusiasm on those handles." In fact, Chandler relates the story of how Coach

Rupp insisted that he and the other pallbearers take a fifth of whiskey with them to the cemetery and drink it in celebration of the good times they had shared. "We asked him," said Chandler, "whether we should drink it on the way out or on the way back, and he said, 'Hell, on the way out, of course. I won't be with ya coming back.'"

• • •

I asked singer/songwriter John Ireson to compose the theme for the *Farewell Baron* documentary, and his lyrics remain an accurate reflection of Rupp's remarkable career.

From the wheat fields of Kansas to the Bluegrass of Kentucky,
Came the son of an immigrant with a legend in his soul
And a spirit so contagious that it spread throughout the country
And the Big Blue Machine began to roll.

Born to be a leader, born to teach, born to win.
His faith and his dreams were strong enough.
   He needed stronger men.
So he lifted up his eyes and found help from the hills.
Gave Kentucky and the world a million thrills.

The year was 1948… the Baron went to war.
His weapon was a basketball, his soldiers would not fall.
They fought the battles one by one and conquered the world
And the Fabulous Five won it all.

He told us of the fiddlers, how they fiddled here and there.
Oh they fiddled and they fiddled till the final score was in.
They were champions in that season, and they gave the Baron reason
To call the fiddlers concert violins.

Then one cruel year brought the shadows of a lifetime
When the Big Machine was tarnished by the weakness of a few,
And his heart was surely broken, but his honor strong as steel
Wouldn't let the world condemn Kentucky Blue.

There was one who stood beside him if he lost or if he won,
A gentle persuasion and a rock behind his fears.
With modesty and beauty soothing all the storms inside him,
Esther loved the Baron over forty years.

No more worlds to conquer. He leaves only memories
Of the battles that the Baron fought and won for me and you.
Though the cheers still resound for the rhapsody in brown,
The Baron's blood was always Big Blue.

Now the Baron's chair is empty. The fans have all gone home.
The silence on the sidelines fills the Coliseum air.
Yet another season opens with the cheering of the Blue,
And the spirit of the Baron will be there.

Farewell Baron, basketball Baron,
Winningest coach that the game ever knew.
Farewell Baron, basketball Baron,
The man who made the world look up to Kentucky Blue.

• • •

Joe B. Hall

PART TWO:

Joe B. Hall

When native Kentuckian Joe B. Hall was named to succeed his mentor as head coach at UK in 1972, he was determined to be his own man and not simply do everything just as Rupp had done. On the day that his appointment was officially announced, Hall was walking back to his car following the news conference when he noticed a huge hairpin on the pavement in the parking lot. Rupp had been famous for his many superstitions. He made sure to step on the same manhole cover outside Memorial Coliseum before every game, but always with his right foot. The team manager always held up three varieties of chewing gum for Rupp to choose from before every game, and Adolph always chose the stick of gum in the middle. The Baron was constantly looking for lucky pennies or hairpins on the day of a game, and Hall was well aware that team managers had often been dispatched to strew pennies and pins in Rupp's path to insure that the old coach would be feeling lucky by game time.

Naturally, when Hall discovered the giant hairpin lying next to his car that day, he assumed someone had intentionally placed it there to get his tenure off to a good start. So after examining the pin, Joe B. merely tossed it aside, got in his car, and drove home. The rest of the story sounds as if it came from *Ripley's Believe It or Not.* Coach Hall recalls, "I got out of the car and was starting to walk into the house, when out of the corner of my eye, I noticed something gleaming on the hood of the car. I went back to take a closer look, and there was that same hairpin I had tossed aside in the Coliseum parking lot."

• • •

JOE B. OR CECIL B.?

That same fall, I had moved to Lexington to take a new job at a local television station, WKYT. Part of my duties included hosting a weekly show with Joe B. Hall. Shortly after we met for the first time, Hall asked for my opinion of his idea of the perfect way to open his very first TV program. He said, "How about if we start with a shot of me walking up to the trophy case in Memorial Coliseum, unlocking it and then reaching in to push the play button on a tape recorder hidden amongst the trophies? Then we hear a voice saying, 'Your mission, Coach Hall, should you choose to accept it, is to replace the winningest coach in the history of college basketball and to maintain the University of Kentucky's unmatched standard of excellence in the sport while adding to its already impressive total of SEC and NCAA championships. This tape will self-destruct in five seconds.' Then we rig a little puff of smoke to go off in the trophy case as I turn and walk down the hall while the theme to the TV show *Mission Impossible* plays in the background."

We constructed the opening just the way Coach Hall envisioned it, and the viewers loved it. Through eight seasons of hosting that weekly show with him, I came to know Joe B. Hall as a man who truly cared about others and loved his university—a man committed to fulfilling his impossible mission with class and dignity, even if it meant ruffling some feathers along the way.

. . .

PAPA BEAR

Hall was nicknamed "Papa Bear" by his players after he spent a night in the bed of star forward Kevin Grevey. The Wildcats had bussed back from a Saturday afternoon game in Starkville, Mississippi, arriving in Lexington about 2 a.m. With another important game looming on Monday, Coach Hall ordered the players to go straight back to the dorm and get to bed immediately. Then while driving home, Hall remembered that Grevey had been complaining of a sore throat and just not feeling well, so he decided to turn around and go back to campus to check on him.

When he got to Grevey's room, Kevin was nowhere to be found, and his roommate, G. J. Smith, meekly offered the suggestion that Grevey might have gone to do some laundry. In reality, Grevey's girlfriend had been there waiting for the bus when it arrived, and Kevin recalls, "There was no way I was just going to kiss her goodnight and say 'See ya later.'" Hall sat down on Grevey's bed and began what would prove to be an all-night vigil. Grevey says, "To this day, I still have visions of Coach Hall snuggling down in my bed while poor ol' G. J. was over there twitching like a leaf in the wind."

Hall finally fell asleep and didn't awaken until almost 7 o'clock, at which time he left a note for his leading scorer that read: "Now that you're back, come to my office to see me. By the way, I kept your bed warm last night."

Coach Hall had recruited the seven "Super Kittens" and had come to admire not just their basketball talents but their zest for life. He says, "There wasn't a bad kid in that bunch, but they were always stirring up some kind of mischief, and I had to keep a tight rein on them."

• • •

STEVE LOCHMUELLER

As punishment for staying out all night, Grevey was suspended for the next game against LSU, and Coach Hall announced that Steve Lochmueller would replace him in the starting lineup. Hall remembers that the air duct between the players' locker room and the coach's dressing quarters conducted sound and made it easy for him and his staff to hear everything being said by the players in the next room. Just prior to that LSU game, he recalls hearing Lochmueller launch into a stirring imitation of Kentucky's famous radio announcer, Cawood Ledford. The big forward's soliloquy went something like this: "Ladies and gentlemen, you can feel the electricity in the air here at Memorial Coliseum tonight as we get ready for the biggest game of the season so far." Lochmueller then announced the Kentucky starters, saving himself for last: "And rounding out the starting lineup, at forward, the pride of Tell City, Indiana, a 6'6" junior, Steeeeeeeeve Lochmueller! The teams are coming to center court now and exchanging handshakes, and we're ready to go. The ball is tossed in the air, and Kentucky wins the tip. Jimmy Dan Connor controls it in backcourt and immediately calls time out. It looks like we're going to get a substitution for Kentucky. Kevin Grevey replaces Steve Lochmueller." Players and coaches on either side of that locker room wall nearly fell down laughing.

• • •

RONNIE LYONS

Ronnie Lyons was a year older than the Super Kittens but equally ornery. Lyons, a Huck Finn lookalike with a mop of blond hair, was also a huge wrestling fan. During the Christmas holidays when the other students were off campus, Hall hired a retired gentleman to handle security for his players at Holmes Hall. The elderly man awoke Hall with a phone call to his home late one night and breathlessly announced, "You've got to get over here, Coach. The boys got to wrasslin' and I think they've killed Jim Duff. He's covered with blood and I'm not sure if he's still breathing or not." The possible corpse was a walk-on player well liked by everyone on the team, and Hall knew instantly that the security guard was being duped. The coach ordered his night watchman to "go back in there and tell Jim Duff to get up, wipe all the ketchup off and get to the phone because Coach Hall wants to talk to him immediately, and tell him to bring Ronnie Lyons with him, because I know whose idea this wrestling match was." More than 25 years later, Lyons still marvels at how Coach Hall was able to figure out every caper the players devised.

• • •

13-13

Hall's second season at Kentucky, 1973-74, was a mystery to all concerned as the talented but undersized Wildcats struggled through a pressure-packed campaign. They took a dismal 12-13 record into the final game of the season against Mississippi State at Memorial Coliseum. Another loss would produce Kentucky's first losing season since 1927. The players on that Wildcat squad remember Joe Hall ignoring the possible blight on the school's glorious record and instead encouraging them to "just go out on that floor and have fun. Forget tradition, forget pressure, and play every minute for the sheer fun of it." Kentucky won that game 108-69 and laid the groundwork for a trip to the Final Four the very next year.

• • •

ALL-AMERICANS GALORE

Washington State coach George Raveling, a notorious banquet speaker with a droll sense of humor, brought his team to Lexington for the University of Kentucky Invitational Tournament in December of 1974. Raveling got up at a pretournament luncheon and said, "I don't feel like eating. Before I came over here, I was reading the Kentucky media guide, and it was scary. We don't have any high school All-Americans on our team at Washington State, but according to that media guide, even the team managers at Kentucky, the kids who wash the jocks, were All-Americans in high school."

• • •

THE TRIP DOWN UNDER

How does a team go 13-13 one year and then come within one victory of the national championship the very next season? Almost every player who suffered through the disappointing 1973-74 season believes the remarkable turnaround had its origin on another continent.

The summer before the 1974-75 season, the Wildcats embarked on a State Department-sponsored Australian tour that required them to play 19 games in 23 days. Rather than sleep in hotels, the players stayed overnight with local families. Center Bob Guyette recalls, "We would get in very late at night after a game and then have an early morning wake-up call to get right back on the road again, so there was very little time to get to know our hosts, and after a few weeks of that hectic schedule and traveling city to city, six guys to a station wagon, our tempers were getting pretty short."

In one game near the end of the tour, UK guard Mike Flynn lost his cool over a bad call, wound up and heaved the ball all the way over the bleachers. Flynn says, "They had to hold up the game for a while to chase down the ball, and it's a wonder I didn't start a riot, but we were all glad to get out of there that night, and our team really was a lot closer-knit after we survived that long grind."

● ● ●

Joe B. Hall and Mike Flynn

BOBBY KNIGHT'S SLAP

December 7, 1974 was Kentucky's own "D-Day" as the Wildcats were demolished in Bloomington by the Indiana Hoosiers. Indiana's veteran center Kent Benson took UK freshmen Rick Robey and Mike Phillips to school that afternoon as Indiana romped to a 98-74 win. With the clock winding down under two minutes, the outcome had long since been decided when Bobby Knight loudly protested a charging call against Hoosier guard Steve Ahlfield.

Joe Hall remembers, "Coach Knight was way down by our bench, and since he and I had always been friends, I just playfully started applauding him and said something like, 'Way to go, Bobby, stay on 'em!' Well, he turned to me and said, 'You coach your team and I'll coach mine.' I didn't want any lasting damage to our relationship, so at that point I stood up and apologized and told him I hadn't meant any harm by my comment."

That should have been the end of the incident, but as Hall turned and started back to his seat on the bench, Knight reached out and slapped him on the back of the head. "When I turned around to see what had happened," said Hall, "Bobby was smiling, and as he reached out as if he wanted to shake hands, I remember him saying, 'I didn't mean anything by that, either.' Then suddenly Lynn got into it."

Lynn was Kentucky assistant coach Lynn Nance, a big, burly former FBI agent who had to be restrained from decking Knight right on the spot. If cooler heads hadn't prevailed, it could have been the ugliest incident in Bob Knight's controversial career.

Today, Joe B. Hall prefers to remember that game as "a great learning experience that woke us up to the kind of physical effort we were going to have to give to be successful."

• • •

REVENGE IN DAYTON

Indiana entered the Mideast Regional Finals that season with a 34-game winning streak and ranked No. 1 in the country. Every Wildcat who saw action that day remembers it as the most physical game he ever played. Coach Hall felt his players hadn't done a good enough job in the earlier game in Bloomington of fighting through all the screens that were such an integral part of the Indiana offense.

At practice the day before that Indiana rematch, Hall threw all the media out of the arena. Bob Knight's former Ohio State teammate, Jerry Lucas, had been assigned by NBC to do the color commentary for the telecast. Everyone assumed at the time that Hall feared Lucas might leak information to Knight, but Joe B. maintains to this day that his clearing of the gym had nothing to do with distrust of Lucas. He just felt there was too much of a circus atmosphere in the building and wanted his players to be spared all of the distractions.

Hall says, "Our first team was just brutalizing the second team in practice that day, so I called off the session after only 15 minutes or so and sent the team back to the hotel. Somebody might have been killed if I hadn't, and I knew our guys were ready."

It was fortunate there were no fatalities in the game the next day. On Indiana's very first trip down the court, their burly forward Steve Green came out to set a high screen on Kentucky's Bob Guyette. The solidly built Guyette, now a successful facial surgeon in Scottsdale, Arizona, might have rearranged Green's facial features by not just fighting through his screen, but by running right over him and knocking Green flat. Guyette was called for a foul on the play, but that may have been the defining moment in the game. Kentucky never backed down all afternoon and won a thriller, 92-90.

In the locker room just prior to the game, Hall had written these words on the blackboard: NETS, BUS, POLICE, COLISEUM. He then cautioned his players to be careful with the scissors while cutting down the nets after winning the game. He related to them how the team bus would be met by the Kentucky Highway Patrol when it crossed the state line and how they would get a police escort all the way to Lexington. He told them how Interstate 75 would be lined with cars that had pulled off the highway for a glimpse of their heroes and how overpasses would be decorated with congratulatory signs. He predicted Lexington police would pick them up on the edge of town and escort them to Memorial Coliseum where thousands of loyal fans would be waiting to honor them.

The scenario played out exactly as Hall had described it, and for years afterward, some of the Kentucky players thought Joe B. Hall must have had a miraculous vision that day. Hall has since revealed the truth. On his post-game radio show, the coach had simply related to announcer Cawood Ledford everything he had predicted to the players. Naturally, the state highway patrol heard it, the fans in their cars on I-75 heard it, the Lexington police heard it, and a good portion of the radio listeners across Kentucky that day headed straight for Memorial Coliseum to welcome home the Mideast Regional champions.

• • •

KEVIN GREVEY

Legendary UCLA coach John Wooden announced his retirement the day before the championship game of the 1975 NCAA tournament against Kentucky. His sideline behavior in the second half of a tight contest might have been bad enough to draw a technical foul for any other coach in America, but there was no way the officials were going to tarnish the swan song of the venerable Wooden.

UCLA forward Dave Meyers wasn't as fortunate. With just over six minutes remaining and UCLA clinging to a one-point lead, Meyers slapped his palm on the floor and shouted, "Dammit!" after being called for a foul against Kevin Grevey. The officials immediately called a technical on Meyers and sent Grevey to the line to shoot what could have been three free throws (a one-and-one plus the technical). Grevey was an excellent foul shooter, but this time he missed both the front end of the one-and-one and the technical.

Kentucky was awarded the ball with a chance to take the lead, but the Wildcats were called for a foul on the inbounds play, and what could have been a five-point swing resulted in no points for Kentucky. UCLA hung on to win its tenth NCAA title in twelve years despite a 34-point performance by Grevey.

Years later, Kevin Grevey ran into Coach Wooden off the court and confronted him, saying, "Coach, I really admire and respect you for all that you've accomplished, but something has been sticking in my craw all these years, and I just have to tell you now that if you hadn't announced your retirement before that final game in '75 and intimidated the officials the way you did, Kentucky would have won that championship."

Grevey remembers the "Wizard of Westwood" breaking into a sly smile and saying, "Son, I've had something I've wanted to tell you all these years, too. If you'd have just played a little defense in that game, Kentucky probably would have beaten us." Grevey says, "I got zinged by the master."

Kevin Grevey had all the skills necessary to be a good defensive player, and he did occasionally perform extremely well at the defensive end of the court. But for most of his four years at Kentucky, Grevey preferred to pour his energy into playing offense, despite constant

Kevin Grevey

prodding from Coach Hall to concentrate on defense as well. One day in practice, Hall blew his whistle, and roared at Grevey, "Which way did your man just go, Kevin?" Grevey got a contemplative look on his face and started visually searching the far reaches of the Coliseum. He appeared to look in every corner of both the lower and upper decks before finally offering his answer, "Coach, I just don't know where he went." Even a strict disciplinarian like Joe B. Hall couldn't stifle his laughter that day.

• • •

NEW YORK, NEW YORK

Seldom has a Kentucky team finished a season on a better roll than the 1975-76 Wildcats did. Their sprint to the finish line was totally unexpected after a Valentine's Day massacre at the hands of Vanderbilt in Nashville left the Cats with a dismal 10-10 record.

Even with second-leading scorer Rick Robey out with a knee injury, Kentucky finished the regular season with six straight wins and gladly accepted an invitation to the NIT in New York. At that time, all NIT games were still being played in Madison Square Garden. Kentucky hadn't ventured there since the gambling scandals of the early 1950s, and almost no one gave them much chance of sticking around the Big Apple too long on this trip.

Wins over Niagara, Kansas State, and Providence propelled the Cats onto center stage for a matchup with UNC-Charlotte in the championship game, and no Broadway show has ever had a more unlikely star than Kentucky's Reggie Warford. The 6'1" senior from the tiny town of Drakesboro, Kentucky, had started only one regular season game in his three-year career at UK. Reggie had not scored a single basket from the field in the first three games of the NIT, and when the title game got underway, Warford was wearing an elastic wrap around his ribcage due to a painful muscle strain suffered during warmups for the semifinals.

The championship game see-sawed back and forth until a 15-foot jumper by Warford finally put Kentucky ahead to stay, 64-63. Almost unbelievably, it was one of seven clutch baskets that night by the frail-looking Reggie Warford. He later said, "I learned what discipline is all about. I don't think I took a bad shot all season, but UNC-Charlotte was sagging in on Mike Phillips, and when that happens the guards have to shoot. I did what I had to do, and now my basketball playing days are all over, but no one can ever take this win away from me."

Kentucky hung to win 71-67, finishing the season with 10 straight wins and an NIT championship.

• • •

THE GAMBLE PAYS OFF

Joe B. Hall may have had the scholarly look of a certified public accountant or perhaps a physics professor, but he definitely had some riverboat gambler in him. When Hall's heavily favored 1978 team shockingly fell behind Florida State by ten points at halftime of their opening game of the NCAA Tournament in Knoxville, Hall benched three of his starters who had played poorly in the first twenty minutes.

Kentucky came back to win by 11, but Joe B. later said, "If it hadn't worked out that way, if my decision had backfired, I couldn't have gone back to Lexington. I would have had to head for the hills because they would have had a posse waiting for me at the city limits."

• • •

KYLE MACY

Kyle Macy was not a native Kentuckian, but bluegrass basketball fans embraced him as they did few other players in the storied history of the program. Macy says he's never been quite able to figure out why he became such a beloved figure at Kentucky, but he offers this theory: "I wasn't very tall. I wasn't very strong. I wasn't very fast. It was easy for the fans to relate to me, especially since they could see that winning meant as much to me as it did to them."

When Macy decided to transfer after spending his freshman year as a starter at Purdue, he remembers having to recruit Kentucky and sell them on the idea. Macy says, "Joe Hall told us that Kentucky didn't like to take transfers and suggested that I might be better off somewhere else, but the more I outlined my reasons for wanting to join the UK program, the more convinced Coach Hall became that it would be a good fit."

It was a perfect fit, as Macy helped lead the Wildcats to a national championship in his very first season wearing blue and white, but first he had to sit out one season as a redshirt. Macy recalls scrimmaging against the varsity each day in practice and thinking that if those "knockdown, drag-out scrimmages were any indication, every Kentucky player would probably foul out of every game that season." Actually that 1976-77 UK squad came within one game of returning to the Final Four, and Macy says, "The experience of going against a very physical, defensive-minded guard like Larry Johnson every day in practice prepared me for all the challenges I faced that next year."

Macy played a big part in the win that sent Kentucky back to the Final Four in 1978. Michigan State, with freshman sensation Earvin "Magic" Johnson, was leading the Wildcats by five points at halftime of the Mideast Regional championship game in Dayton. Kyle says, "We had actually left the locker room and were on our way back out to the court when I noticed Coach Hall and

Kyle Macy

assistant coach Leonard Hamilton talking strategy in the tunnel. They called Rick Robey and me over and suggested that Rick come out to the high post and set screens for me against their matchup zone defense. It got me open for some jumpers, and they also fouled me a lot."

Did they ever! Macy made 10 straight free throws in the second half as Kentucky came back to win a low-scoring game, 52-49. Macy says he ran into Magic Johnson many times over the next several years and never failed to remind Magic of the outcome in that game.

• • •

MEET ME IN ST. LOUIE

The national media seemed reluctant to praise the 1977-78 Kentucky Wildcats. Reporters and writers ignored the hard work and dedication that had produced a 29-2 record heading into the NCAA championship game and focused instead on the absence of smiles on the players' faces. They repeatedly referred to Kentucky's "season without joy" or "season without celebration." Rather than dreaming up the kind of colorful nicknames that had been bestowed on Rupp's best teams, the media stuck this squad with uncomplimentary labels like "The Slaughterhouse Five" and "Joe's Robots."

Kentucky played Arkansas in the semifinals at the Checkerdome in St. Louis, and Joe Hall's loyal assistant,

Dicky Parsons, says the coaching staff felt the Razorbacks were the most talented team in the country with the possible exception of Kentucky. "In fact," says Parsons, "we didn't even show the players any film of Arkansas, because we didn't want them to know just how good they were."

After the Wildcats got by the Hogs, 64-59, Hall stood at the door of the locker room and repeated the message, "No celebrating," as the players filed past him, fueling even more suspicion in the national media.

Today, Joe Hall looks back on that day and flashes a knowing smile as he says, "The Duke players threw their coach, Bill Foster, into the showers after their semifinal win over Notre Dame, but I told our players 'If you're running a marathon and you're leading after the first mile, you don't stop to celebrate.'"

The night before the championship game, Hall suggested that his players go see a good movie well outside the city limits of St. Louis where no one would badger them about basketball. But senior center Rick Robey informed Hall that the players had talked it over and preferred to stay in and watch a tape of Duke's semifinal win over Notre Dame. Robey and the other seniors on the squad felt they had too much fun in San Diego as freshmen when they lost in the finals to UCLA.

The tension in the locker room, though, was stifling as the players prepared to meet Duke for the title. The message was clear. Only a victory could keep this edition of the Wildcats from being labeled a failure.

In that supercharged atmosphere, Joe B. Hall began his pregame talk to the team. As he cautioned them not to succumb to the pressure, he purposely messed up his neatly combed hair and rolled onto the training table writhing like a snake, eventually wrapping himself around one of the legs of the table, and finally stepping directly into a large garbage can. Unfortunately, there were no reporters around to hear the laughter that rippled through the room. The tension had been broken.

As for the game itself that night, well, it belonged to a smooth Kentucky lefty named Jack Givens. Hall had recruited Givens from his own backyard in Lexington along with Jack's boyhood friend, James Lee, who still shakes his head in disbelief as he discusses the phenomenal shooting display Givens put on against Duke. "I had seen Jack get hot before," says Lee, "but that night he was on fire."

An almost impossible bank shot from the right corner was the highlight of Givens's incredible 41-point performance. "When that thing went in," says Givens, "I knew it was our night and there was no way we were going lose."

With the outcome no longer in doubt, Hall pulled his starters but quickly sent most of them back in when Duke managed to draw within four points with 10 seconds remaining. Blue Devils coach Bill Foster called a timeout to set up his pressure defense, but Kentucky beat it with a long pass downcourt to James Lee, the other homegrown Wildcat, who put a fitting exclamation point on the Kentucky's 94-88 win. "Every player dreams about getting to take the last shot in a championship game, and dunks were kinda my specialty," recalls Lee, "so I threw it down in a way they'd remember."

• • •

Jack Givens

HOW GOOD WERE THEY?

Kyle Macy has never wavered in his belief that the 1978 NCAA champions were one of the best teams in the history of college basketball. "We may not have been the best of all time," argues Macy, "but I really can't think of any that were much better. We could beat you in so many different ways. The Twin Towers [Robey and Phillips] created special problems for any defense, and the rest of us could all score. We also had the ability to adapt to whatever situation came up. I hope history will be kinder to us as the years go by."

• • •

GREAT IN ANY LANGUAGE

In an exhibition game prior to that unforgettable 1977-78 season, the Cats beat a talented team from the Soviet Union 109-75. Alexander Gomelsky, the normally cocky Soviet coach, appeared downright shellshocked afterwards as he told reporters in his broken English, "Kentucky best team I ever look."

• • •

CHRIS GETTELFINGER

Kentucky and Tennessee first met on the basketball court in 1910, and the intensity of their rivalry has been building ever since. Chris Gettelfinger grew up in Knoxville, Tennessee, where he became a high school basketball star. He was well aware of the resentment in Knoxville toward the Big Blue Machine some three hours to the north. Many Tennessee fans could go a lifetime without ever saying a good word about Kentucky basketball, but Gettelfinger, a hustling guard as fiery as the red hair on his head, had attended summer basketball camps in Lexington and developed a healthy respect for the UK program. He still planned to play at Tennessee, but two unexpected factors brought about a change of plans.

Gettelfinger came down with a case of mononucleosis during his senior year of high school, and highly respected Vols coach Ray Mears retired. Tennessee then recruited one of Gettelfinger's schoolboy rivals, Bert Bertelkamp, and Chris shocked his Knoxville neighbors by electing to play at Kentucky instead. Many labeled him a traitor and sent him nasty letters, but Gettelfinger now says, "For the most part, it was a positive type of jealousy. Many of my friends gradually turned into Kentucky fans and came to admire UK's great basketball tradition. I knew that tradition would still be flourishing 50 years later, whereas Tennessee might always be known as a football school. And on top of that, I absolutely fell in love with the Lexington lifestyle, with all the beautiful horse farms and the rolling countryside, going to the races at Keeneland and just soaking in the admiration of the fans."

Chris Gettelfinger never became a starter at UK, but interestingly enough he did become one of the fans' favorites in Lexington. Toward the end of every lopsided game, they would chant his name, exhorting Coach Joe B. Hall to give him some playing time. Gettelfinger puts that development in perspective today. "Lots of people tend to live their lives through the athletes they admire," says Chris, "and I was them. They knew I was the kind of unselfish player who understood his role and was willing to sacrifice for the good of the team, and they could identify with that attitude."

One of Gettelfinger's most vivid memories is from the spring following the national championship season in 1978. "All of the players," says Chris, "were just worn out from that pressure-packed campaign and the circus atmosphere that surrounded it. We were all anxious to get away from basketball for a while and kind of recharge our batteries, but then Coach Hall informed us that he had arranged a summer trip to Japan where we would be playing a series of exhibition games. Coach really wanted to make a great impression on the Japanese people, and so two weeks later he had us practicing in 90-degree heat inside Memorial Coliseum with no air conditioning. The players started grumbling about how badly we needed a vacation from basketball and how none of us really wanted to go to Japan. Joe B. got word of our grumbling and called a team meeting to put the trip to a vote. We talked about it among ourselves, and decided to hang together and vote against going. But before Coach Hall asked for a show of hands, he let us know how disappointed in us he was and how he wouldn't soon forget our lack of dedication.

"Poor old Scott Courts, a reserve center who had clashed with the coaches in the past, just happened to be standing at the front of the cluster of players. When Joe B. finally asked for a show of hands from anyone who didn't want to go, Scott couldn't see all of us behind him giving in one by one and keeping our hands at our sides. Scott threw his hand in the air and said, 'Coach, I would much rather just go back home to Colorado for the summer and forget about basketball for a while.' Coach Hall promptly informed him that since he was the only player who felt that way, he could just stay behind, and the rest of us would go to Japan without him. To this day, I still feel bad for Scott Courts. By the time we got back from Japan, he had transferred to another school."

Gettelfinger returned to Knoxville to live after graduation. He married a local girl and turned her into a Kentucky fan. She even bought their two-year-old son a blue and white warmup suit. When the Wildcats visited Knoxville for a game late in the 2002 season, the Gettelfingers decided to take their six-year-old daughter along to the arena. As they were walking out the door, Chris turned back to see his tiny son standing on the stairway all dressed in blue and white and waving a Kentucky shaker. The tradition continues.

• • •

THE FANTASTIC FINISH

Wiping out a seven-point deficit in the final 31 seconds of a game may not sound like a tremendous feat in this era of the three-point shot, but when the Wildcats did it in December of 1978 to pull out a victory over Kansas, it was considered downright miraculous.

With just those 31 seconds left in overtime, the unbeaten and fifth-ranked Jayhawks led Kentucky 66-60 behind the brilliant 27-point performance of Darnell Valentine. Dwight Anderson, a lightning-quick freshman guard, scored the next four points for Kentucky on a layup and two free throws, but with only 10 ticks of the clock left, Kansas still had the ball out of bounds under their own basket with a two-point lead. Everyone in Rupp Arena knew that if the Jayhawks got the ball inbounds, Kentucky would have to foul, but Anderson somehow got his hand on the inbounds pass. With an almost superhuman effort, he saved the ball from going out of bounds and batted it all the way across the court to Kyle Macy.

The stunned crowd watched Macy drain a 15-foot jumper that tied the game with four seconds left. Then something even more bizarre happened. Even though Kansas had already used its last time-out, Valentine signaled for another one. The officials immediately called a technical foul that sent the always-cool Macy to the line to shoot a potential game-winning free throw.

Kyle Macy was one of the best free-throw shooters in the country, partly because he never varied his preshot routine. Macy's own description of the routine goes like this: "First I would line up my toe right in the middle of the free-throw stripe. Then I would dry my fingers by reaching down and grabbing both socks. Then it was dribble three times, take a deep breath, bend at the knees a little more than most free-throw shooters, sight the basket and let it go."

This time the routine almost failed him. His potential game-winning toss against Kansas seemed to be slightly off target. Macy says, "I had to use some body English and almost walk it in." The shot finally dropped, and Kentucky owned one of the most unlikely victories in its long history.

That game's place in Kentucky lore has grown in stature with each passing year. Macy says, "Rupp Arena seats about 23,000, but over the years, I bet I've had 50,000 people tell me they were there that night in 1978."

• • •

THE BIG ONE THAT GOT AWAY

In 1979, Kentucky made an all-out effort to recruit Virginia schoolboy sensation Ralph Sampson, one of the most sought after players in the history of high school basketball. With the nation eagerly awaiting his decision, Sampson was taking his own sweet time about it. In fact, most schools had already completed their recruiting and

Kentucky had signed five players, including Pennsylvania phenom Sam Bowie, who, at seven feet tall, would be dwarfed by Sampson, who was nearly four inches taller. Joe B. Hall and his staff were doing their best to convince Ralph that his addition to their already star-studded cast of recruits could make for one of the strongest college basketball teams ever, perhaps even eclipsing the great UCLA teams of the Lew Alcindor era.

Finally came word from Sampson's hometown of Harrisonburg, Virginia, that he was ready to hold a news conference announcing his chosen school. The following morning, I flew to Harrisonburg in a small chartered plane and took a quick tour of the town before heading to the high school gymnasium where Ralph was scheduled to meet the media. Outside the Claude E. Warren Fieldhouse was a sign that read "Home of the Proud Blue Streaks." It was difficult to imagine the gangly Sampson "streaking" down the court, but everything about the news conference that day would turn out to be almost unimaginable.

I will never forget the sight of young Sampson ducking to get through the doorway leading into the gym where a section of bleachers had been pulled out on one side of the court to accommodate all the reporters and well wishers. A table and five chairs had been set up facing the horde. Ralph was accompanied to the table by his mother and his father, who was dressed in a natty pinstriped suit and looked like a miniature edition of his already famous offspring. The school's athletic director welcomed everyone and then warned us not to ask any questions about the job status of Harrisonburg basketball coach Bill Bergey, who couldn't be missed, sitting next to Ralph in an iridescent yellow sportcoat.

Then came the moment everyone had been waiting for. Sampson cleared his throat, swallowed hard, and said, "It's been a tough decision for me, and uh, the last couple of days, I didn't know what to do. I've changed my mind at least 50 times. Came down to Kentucky and Virginia, so I think I'm going with ... Virginia." There was an audible gasp from the crowd and a soft cheer that sounded almost as tentative as the young superstar's commitment. Reporters looked at each other in disbelief. Had we heard him correctly? Had he actually said, "I *think* I'm going with Virginia."? Finally, a reporter said, "It sounds like you're leaving the door open to change your mind. Could that still happen?" Ralph smiled in a shy, almost embarrassed way and replied, "It could happen. Yeah, I'm leaving it open." I remember asking him at that point, "Ralph, if you do change your mind, will you invite all of us back here for another news conference?" I admit now it was kind of a smart-aleck question, but this gentle giant didn't seem to read any sarcasm into it. He simply nodded and said, "Yeah, I will."

Sampson went on to explain that he would not sign with Virginia that day or the next. Someone interrupted him to ask, "If Joe Hall were to call and try to talk you out of ever signing with Virginia, would you talk to him?" Ralph's incredibly long frame clearly squirmed in the chair as he answered, "I don't know. It depends on how I feel." The veteran writers in the group weren't about to let him off that easy. One asked, "Why did you take so long to make your decision?" Ralph's frustration with the proceedings began to show as he snapped, "Because I didn't know where I wanted to go until now." At that point, I think it dawned on all of us that this man-child was being brutally honest with us. He had actually called a news conference without knowing what his decision was, presumably because someone had convinced him it was time to announce something, anything. Then, from the back of the bleachers came another logical question. "Exactly when did you finally make up your mind?" The answer provided a fitting conclusion to a most confusing day. "This morning I was still undecided. Uh, I was, uh, changing back and forth all day. Kentucky was number one on my list for a while. For the people back there, uh, I haven't signed yet, but I'll probably be going to Virginia."

History confirms that Ralph Sampson did go to Virginia where he became arguably the dominant player of his era in college basketball. Kentucky fans now can only wonder how many more national championship trophies might reside in the Bluegrass if Sampson had changed his mind one more time those many years ago.

• • •

DICKY BEAL

If there was another guard in the Joe Hall era who captured the hearts of the fans the way Macy did, it had to be Dicky Beal, a 5'10" dynamo from Covington, Kentucky. Multiple knee surgeries had limited Dicky's effectiveness as he limped through the early stages of his senior year in 1984. "I was never 100 percent that year," says Beal. "But with all the talent on that team, I didn't feel I had to be completely healthy. We just needed somebody who could penetrate and spread the ball around and play solid defense. I could still do all those things, but not quite as well as Coach Hall wanted me to. He knew I was having trouble getting full range of motion with my knee."

Hall was so concerned that he called the surgeon who had operated on Dicky's knee, Dr. James Andrews, in Columbus, Georgia, and asked if adhesions in that knee could be slowing Beal down. "The doctor said if Dicky hadn't been favoring it, the adhesions should have been broken down by that time," recalls Hall. "I finally asked Dr. Andrews if it would do any further damage to the knee if we just grabbed Dicky's ankle and snapped it back against his thigh to try to break those adhesions. When he said it was worth a try, I walked right up to Dicky on the training table, told him to relax, and then just pulled that lower leg down through a full range of motion. Dicky let out a blood-curdling scream and looked at me like I was crazy, but from that day on, he started moving better."

Dicky Beal today is grateful to Joe B. Hall for much more than just that training table magic. "Coach Hall never got his due," says Beal. "He was a great coach and a great man, and look at the kind of men he turned out. He really tried to shape us into good people, and I'm especially grateful for the way he set my direction in life."

Dicky Beal

Beal didn't even blame Hall for some incredibly grueling practices following a loss to Tennessee in the last game of the 1984 regular season. "Coach did the right thing," says Beal. "We were playing sluggish, and those practices woke us up. I thought every practice during my career at Kentucky was tough, but those were really painful."

Dicky Beal still remembers as if it were yesterday the pain of being elbowed in the nose by teammate Sam Bowie in the championship game of the Mideast Regional against Illinois. "It wasn't Sam's fault. I had no business being underneath the basket with all those big guys, but I missed a shot and tried to get my own rebound. The next thing I knew I was seeing stars. He really stunned me." Beal had to leave the game, but after less than a minute on the bench, he was screaming at Coach Hall to put him back in. When Dicky returned, he played some of the best basketball of his career to lead the Cats to victory. Beal was named the tournament MVP.

He had come a long way from his freshman year when Dicky wasn't sure he would even make it through his first game. When he went to the free-throw line for the first time in front of 23,000 fans at Rupp Arena, Beal says, "My knees were actually buckling. I wasn't sure I could stand up long enough to shoot the free throw. It was like one of those cartoons where you see the guy's knees knocking together, only this was real, man."

What happened to Dicky Beal and the Wildcats in the 1984 NCAA championship game against Georgetown in Seattle's Kingdome was downright *un*real. Kentucky led Patrick Ewing and company by seven points at halftime, but the Cats inexplicably made only three of 33 shots in the second half and lost by 13. "It was just one of those strange phenomena that happen," laments Beal. "There is no doubt in my mind that we had the better team, but basketball is crazy sometimes. The next year, Villanova made practically every shot they took against Georgetown, and I'm not sure which is more weird, the fact that they made so many shots or the fact that we missed so many."

• • •

KENNY WALKER

Kenny "Sky" Walker will never forget Joe B. Hall's last game as Kentucky's coach. It was the 1985 West Regional semifinal against St. John's. Walker sets the stage for that matchup. "We really had no business being in the tournament that year. It was probably just the great Kentucky tradition that earned us a bid, but then Coach Hall did a masterful job of coaching and we upset both Washington and UNLV in the early rounds. Coach was really relaxed throughout the postseason. I guess he knew he was going to retire, but even though I had heard some rumors, it was still difficult for me to imagine anybody else as the coach at Kentucky. That was the highest scoring season of my career because Coach Hall put the ball

Kenny Walker

in my hands and let me do my thing."

Walker got off to a great start against St. John's, but their All-American Chris Mullen tried to knock the ball out of Kenny's hands midway through the first half and poked him in the eye instead. Walker's cornea was scratched and his vision was blurry the rest of the night. In fact, by the second half, the eye had nearly swollen shut, and although Kenny finished with a team-high 23 points, St. John's claimed an 86-70 win.

On his postgame radio show, Hall announced his retirement, saying, "I've done what I wanted to do. I've done it where I wanted to do it with the people I wanted to do it with."

Kenny Walker, who started doing postgame radio commentary himself during the 2000 UK season, says, "Coach Hall taught me to be responsible and to do charitable things. My ability to relate to people in an easy, relaxed way today is a direct result of Coach Hall's influence."

• • •

Cawood Ledford

CAWOOD LEDFORD

For years, Kentucky players and broadcasters had a difficult time performing at the University of Florida's cramped Alligator Alley. One night, the Wildcats' legendary play-by-play announcer, Cawood Ledford, apologized to his faithful radio listeners by turning to his broadcast partner Ralph Hacker and saying, "Ralph, I would like to be able to tell the folks what happened on that play, but the Florida cheerleaders were shaking their fuzzy things right in front of us." Hacker merely deadpanned, "Pom poms, Cawood, pom poms."

• • •

RALPH HACKER

Hacker spent 20 years as Cawood Ledford's sidekick before taking over the play-by-play duties for the 1992-93 season. He remembers his mentor was always brutally honest in his description of the games. "One night we were going to be a little late coming back from a commercial just before tipoff, so I called referee Burrell Crowell over and asked him if he would mind holding up the action for 30 seconds, and his reply was, 'Would you have Cawood say something good about me?' Cawood overheard the question, and he just looked up and said, 'Let's go, throw up the damn ball.'"

Many of Hacker's most vivid memories of his years with Ledford have to do with Cawood's willingness to criticize bad calls by the officials. "I'll never forget the night we were playing Tennessee in Knoxville and Larry Steele tried to drive the lane for a basket," says Hacker. "Tennessee's big center Tom Boerwinkle knocked Steele all the way into the bleachers, and unbelievably, the official, Butch Lambert, called a charging foul on Larry. Cawood just went crazy, blasting the call and chastising Lambert for his horrible judgment. Not long after that during a game at Auburn, Butch Lambert again was officiating, and he came over to our courtside table during a break in the action and said, 'Cawood, my wife is a big Kentucky fan; she listens to all the games on the radio. Did you really say the call I made at the Alabama game in Memorial Coliseum last month was the worst you ever saw?' Cawood looked Lambert right in the eye and said, 'Yes, I did, but you already topped that at Tennessee the other night.'"

Hacker's courtside seat was close enough to the coaches for him to overhear some memorable comments through the years. He says, "Kentucky was playing North Carolina one night at Freedom Hall in Louisville, and Joe Hall just went berserk over a bad call. He was jumping up and down right in front of us, and finally he took off his coat and just started stomping on it. When his tirade finally ended, he looked back at Cawood and me and said, 'Shoot, I just remembered my glasses are in that coat.'"

• • •

THROUGH THE GRAPEVINE

Many stories were repeated to me by a number of different players, none of whom were willing to be quoted for this book but all of whom swore the stories were true. One such story involved a player living in the Wildcat Lodge in the 1970s. His pretty and petite girlfriend paid him a surprise visit one night, and she was still in the room after the one o'clock curfew had come and gone.

When other team members, aware of the female visitor's presence, saw bed check being conducted by one of the coaches, they assumed the whole team would be required to run sprints at five o'clock the next morning. But when the coach left the room where the girl was known to be, nothing was said. Curious as to how the offending player had gotten away with this breach of team rules, players made their way to his room and demanded an explanation. The player simply pulled out one of the large drawers in his dresser to reveal his girlfriend crammed inside.

• • •

MAGIC JOHNSON

In 2010, Rupp Arena became the place for many luminaries to come and watch the Wildcats' amazing basketball squad. Lebron was there, as was rapper Drake and Pittsburgh Steelers World Champion coach Mike Tomlin. Most wanted to see John Wall.

Magic Johnson was no different.

The former Laker point guard was invited to Kentucky to help the Governor promote a new reading program for inner-city youth. While in Lexington, Magic came to Rupp Arena to watch Wall. While Magic was there he reflected on his time as a collegian, and he credited the UK program with helping his 1979 Michigan State Spartans win their championship.

In 1978, Kyle Macy and company faced Magic's Spartans in the regional finals with a Final Four trip on the line. While the game was close throughout, Kentucky pulled away late, hitting free throws for a 52-49 win. It made an impression on the freshman Magic, who was held in check with just six points and four fouls.

"Watching that Kentucky team, they were so professional," Magic said in 2010. "We learned how to really focus and zero in by watching how they won the championship that season. They were no-nonsense. Of course they were talented, with Goose Givens and Macy and Robey, but they had an attitude—and in 1979 our team tried to be that way, too."

It worked. Magic led his team to the 1979 national title over Larry Bird's Indiana State squad.

"We looked up to that Kentucky team," he said. "They beat us that year. They were the champs."

• • •

Eddie Sutton

PART THREE:

Eddie Sutton

When Joe Hall retired following the 1985 season, Eddie Sutton was tapped as his successor. Sutton had taken a struggling Arkansas program and turned it into a Southwest Conference powerhouse. He inherited a Kentucky team that had too many guards and not enough centers following the graduation of twin towers Sam Bowie and Melvin Turpin.

All Sutton did was install a three-guard offense, with 6'8" senior forward Kenny Walker the tallest player in the lineup. That undersized group surprised even themselves by going 17-1 in SEC play to notch the school's 36th conference championship and finished the season ranked third in both the major wire service polls with a 32-4 record.

Walker still thinks that if that team had been blessed with a true center, it might have added another NCAA championship trophy to the Kentucky collection. "Six-foot-seven-inch Winton Bennett and myself had to go to war every night on the inside," says Walker, "but if we had had a good big man in the middle to free me up to use my athleticism outside the paint, that team really could have won it all."

Sutton had no tolerance for sloppy play, and Kenny Walker vividly recalls a game against Georgia in which the Cats played well for much of the contest but then squandered almost all of a big lead before finally winning by five. "Afterwards, Coach Sutton told us to get dressed and head straight over to Memorial Coliseum for an 11 p.m. practice. My parents were in town, and they would always wait for me outside the locker room and then we'd go out and get something to eat. I remember walking out that night and telling them to go on without me because I had to go to practice. I think Coach Sutton was just trying to get our attention."

• • •

EDDIE, MEET ADOLPH

Sutton himself remembers one incident early in his career that captured his attention like none other. Eddie was an eager and ambitious high school coach in Tulsa in the 1960s. The basketball coaches' association held its annual meeting at the site of the NCAA championship, which was in St. Louis that particular year. Sutton's college coach, Henry Iba, invited Eddie to tag along with him and Curt Gowdy, the renowned broadcaster who got his start calling Oklahoma State basketball games.

Sutton recalls, "I had access to the hospitality suite at the convention hotel just because I was one of Iba's boys.

I'll never forget walking into that room filled with all the great coaches of the day. All of a sudden, there's a commotion in one corner of the room. I walk over there, and down on the floor, arguing about some technical point, I see Coach Iba and Coach Adolph Rupp, two of the most respected coaching legends of that or any other era in college basketball."

What made the scene really memorable for Sutton were the props being used by these two giants of the profession in which Eddie hoped to make his own lasting impression some day. "They've got Coke bottles and 7-Up bottles there on the floor in front of them. The Coke bottles represented Mr. Iba's defense, and the 7-Up bottles were Mr. Rupp's offense. And I hear Mr. Iba say, 'Naw, Adolph, this'll work…' Here were two of the greatest coaching minds in history down on their hands and knees going at it over how some offense or defense would or wouldn't work. You just knew that the one who had the chalk last was going to win."

• • •

THE CREAM GAME

The highlight of Eddie Sutton's short tenure at Kentucky was a 34-point trouncing of in-state rival Louisville on the Cardinals' home court in December of 1986.

It was the worst defeat any Louisville team had ever suffered under Denny Crum.

When Kentucky played Louisville in the Mideast Regional final in 1983, basketball fanatics throughout the state referred to it as "The Dream Game." Despite their close proximity, the schools had not met on the basketball court since 1959. Joe B. Hall had resisted all efforts to get Louisville on the Wildcats' regular season schedule, and in that unavoidable postseason matchup, Louisville beat Hall's Cats 80-68.

Denny Crum's team was the defending national champion when the rivalry was renewed on that cold night in 1986, which was also the first year for the three-point shot. Kentucky made the most of the new rule by bombing in 11 three-pointers, compared to only one for Louisville.

Ed Davender, a savy junior guard from New York City, made his first long-range shot that night en route to a 15-point performance, and that seemed to open the floodgates for the Wildcats. Freshman Rex Chapman made five of eight three-point attempts and finished with a game-high 26 points. Ed Davender remembers it as "Rex's coming-out party.

"He got in a zone that night and his confidence just shot up. After practice one night at Memorial Coliseum, the maintenance people were getting the building ready for a game that night between Lexington Henry Clay and Rex's high school team, Owensboro Appollo. I decided to stick around and watch, and Rex had a super game. He even made a game-winning 40-foot shot at the buzzer, and I knew right then that if he came to Kentucky, he would make an immediate impact on our team."

Ed Davender

Chapman and all the other Kentucky starters got fervent hugs from an uncharacteristically giddy Eddie Sutton as they came to the bench after completing their demolition of the Cardinals. Davender recalls, "We saved Coach Sutton's bacon that night, because in his comments to the press before the game he had referred to Louisville as 'the little brother' when it came to basketball in the state of Kentucky. We played so well that it took him completely off the hook."

• • •

MR. WILDCAT

The only constant in the last five coaching eras at Kentucky has been equipment manager Bill Keightley. A former full-time postal worker now in his fifth decade of seeing to the players' equipment needs, this likeable septuagenarian has been a loyal friend and confidante to whomever has carried the title of basketball coach at Kentucky. He is now such a recognizable figure on the UK bench that fans refer to him as Mr. Wildcat.

Keightley remembers Sutton's unshakeable confidence during time-outs at critical junctures late in games. "If we had a chance to win on our final possession, Eddie would call time and then just stroll casually in front of the bench as the players wondered what was going on. It seemed like he was never going to get around to diagramming a play, but finally he would come over and kneel in the huddle just patting down that frizzy hair of his, and then he would tell the guys to run their offense. He would say whoever gets the open shot is gonna knock it down. It was like he didn't want to put too much pressure on any one player's shoulders. He really gave the whole team a sense of calm, and it almost always seemed to work."

• • •

Editor's Note: This story was written in 2002. Mr. Bill Keightley passed away in 2008.

Rick Pitino

PART FOUR:

Rick Pitino

When Rick Pitino left the NBA's New York Knicks to take over Kentucky's probation-strapped program in the summer of 1989, he quickly came to admire Bill Keightley for his loyalty and his total devotion to Kentucky basketball. Before the season began, Pitino asked Keightley, "Where do you normally sit during the games?" Keightley replied, "Down on the end of the bench beside the trainer."

To the equipment manager's surprise, Pitino told him, "We're gonna change that. I want you to come up and sit beside me." Keightley was honored by the suggestion but stewed over the proposed change for days.

Finally, he went to assistant coach Ralph Willard and asked him what he should do up there beside the head man. Should he talk to Rick or remain quiet? Willard advised Keightley to make sure that Pitino didn't wander out of the coaching box and get any technical fouls.

In the second game of the season against Indiana at the Hoosier Dome, the undermanned Wildcats found themselves within two points of IU in the closing minutes. A ref's call went against Indiana at that point, and an enraged Bob Knight charged out of the coaching box to confront the officials.

Rick Pitino was livid that Knight seemed to be getting away with his tirade without drawing a technical, so he promptly sprinted up the sidelines to where the confrontation was taking place and started offering his own opinion.

Ralph Willard called to Keightley, "You better go get him. We can't afford a technical at this point." So Keightley dutifully trooped up the sidelines, put his arm on Pitino's shoulder, and said softly, "You're out of the coaching box, Rick. You better come on back with me." Keightley recalls that whenever Pitino was really upset, he used to send spit flying all over the place when he talked. In this instance, Pitino whirled around and shouted at Keightley, "Sit yourself back down and shut the [blank] up!" Bill Keightley, one of the kindest, gentlest men on earth, recalls being covered with spit as he turned and went back to the bench to tell Ralph Willard, "I don't believe I'm qualified for this job."

Players, coaches and support staff alike agree that Pitino never held a grudge and after incidents like that one acted as if nothing had happened. Today, Bill Keightley says, "I still love him like a son."

• • •

Sean Woods

Sean Woods remembers vividly the 40-minute meeting that Rick Pitino held with the players the day he was announced as the new Kentucky coach. Woods says, "Coach was there waiting for us in the training room as we straggled in one by one. We could see he was mentally measuring each one of us as we walked by him: 6'3", 6'4", 6'7". When the last guy had entered the room, Coach Pitino asked us, 'Where are all the tall guys? I'm using to working with Patrick Ewing, and none of you guys would come up to his chin.'

"But then he launched into one of the most exciting talks I had ever heard. He told us we were going to win and win right away, and there was just something about the way he said it that made you believe him." Pitino also outlined his pressing, up-tempo style that day and warned the players they would have to be in better physical shape than every team they played.

Later that summer, Woods returned from the Olympic Festival in Norman, Oklahoma, and dropped by Pitino's office to get to know him better. Pitino excitedly introduced him to Rock Oliver, the man he had just hired as his strength and conditioning coach. Woods says, "It was obvious that this Oliver guy was salivating over the opportunity to get started putting the players through their paces, and I was the only player around at that moment." Sean Woods was about to become Rock Oliver's personal guinea pig.

Sean Woods

Woods recalls, "Rock wanted to know if I was willing to go through a little workout for him, and I figured I was safe when I told him I didn't have any gear with me. But he spent about half an hour rummaging around looking for a key to equipment manager Bill Keightley's room and finally found me some stuff to put on. Then he took me out on the court and introduced me to one of his 'coach buddies,' a machine kind of like a lawn mower except that pushing that thing was like pushing a car in neutral. Rock said, 'Let's see if you can push it the length of the court down and back 18 times.' I was dying after about five times, but I wasn't about to let my new conditioning coach know it. I just sucked it up and kept pushing.

"Finally, after the 18th trip down and back," says Woods, "Rock and I walked over to the side of the court to sit down, and as he talked, I kept feeling sicker and sicker. I was afraid I might upchuck all over the guy, and I couldn't help but notice a garbage can on the other side of the court that was starting to look like an oasis in the desert. I made an excuse about needing to be somewhere and nonchalantly started walking toward the other side of the court. It was all I could do to keep from breaking into a sprint, but I couldn't let Rock know how desperate I was. I just barely made it to that garbage can in time to throw up my lunch. I left the gym that day knowing my teammates and I were in for the most grueling preseason camp of our lives."

• • •

DERON FELDHAUS

Pitino's first Kentucky team finished 14-14, but they were in every single game except for a 55-point drubbing at Kansas. The very next season the Cats went 22-6 and compiled the No. 1 record in the SEC, although conference rules prohibited using the word "champion" in conjunction with a team on probation. Deron Feldhaus, a muscular 6'7" forward and the son of a former Wildcat, Alan Feldhaus, remembers the tremendous feeling of accomplishment when that 1990-91 squad was presented with rings inscribed with the words "Back on Top."

"Just the fact that we had come so far after losing 19 games only two years before really made it special. I don't think any of us then could have dreamed about having the best record in the SEC, but that team just became so close, and we all cared about one another," says Feldhaus.

"John Pelphrey, Richie Farmer, Sean Woods and myself all came from very supportive, close knit families and tended to think alike. Sean kinda had a brain cramp one night at Mississippi State when we were losing by three points in the closing seconds. Instead of trying a three-point shot to tie it, he drove in and made a layup. Naturally, we lost by one and afterwards in the locker room, guys were throwing their shoes at him, but we all knew that Woodsy would bounce back and make big plays for us when we needed him. Everything that happened just seemed to draw us closer."

Deron Heldhaus

Dealing with Rick Pitino's volatile temper required a group effort. Feldhaus laughs about it now as he says, "Coach Pitino had a habit of grabbing the side of your stomach and twisting it. One time Pelphrey and I were standing side by side and he got us both at once. We walked into the shower together later and both of us had these big bruises on our sides."

Deron Feldhaus learned not to let Pitino's caustic comments bruise his ego. "Coach was always getting on me about my short arms," says Deron. "He called me Alligator Arms, but it just always made me more determined to prove to him that despite my shortcomings, I was a winner."

Feldhaus had a hard time at first adjusting to the role of sixth man that former Kentucky star Frank Ramsey had popularized with the Boston Celtics. "But I finally realized," Deron says, "that when I went in the game, everybody else was tired and I was fresh. I learned to enjoy the role, and finally on Senior Night when Coach Pitino asked me if I wanted to start for a change, I said, 'Heck, no. Let's not change a thing.'"

• • •

JAMAL MASHBURN

Current NBA star Jamal Mashburn was a three-time All-SEC performer at Kentucky and a consensus All-American in 1993. When Rick Pitino successfully recruited Mashburn out of Cardinal Hayes High School in New York, another prominent New York City coach, Bob Oliva of Christ the King High School, told reporters, "It was like giving an atomic bomb to a terrorist."

• • •

THE GAME OF THE CENTURY

No one could stop the 1991-92 Kentucky Wildcats from calling themselves SEC champions. With everything falling into place that season, some of Pitino's players began consulting a ouija board.

Everything the ouija board predicted seemed to come true. It even confirmed the color of the car driven by one player's girlfriend. When asked if Kentucky would win the SEC tournament, the ouija board responded positively, and sure enough, on March 15, 1992, the Cats demolished Alabama 80–54 in the tournament's championship game.

**Jamal Mashburn grabs a rebound in
"The Game of the Century"**

Yet another ouija board prophecy that Kentucky would meet Duke in the NCAA tournament came true on March 28th in what most basketball experts now refer to as "the Game of the Century." The final score of the East Regional title game was 104–103, and yet players and coaches from both teams still insist some great defense was played that day. Players just kept making difficult shots with a hand in their faces. When Sean Woods finally banked in an incredible shot just over the outstretched arm of Duke's Christian Laettner to give Kentucky a 103-102 lead with only 2.1 seconds to go, Woods and practically everyone else in Philadelphia's Spectrum thought the game was over.

Duke called a time-out during which Kentucky players later said Pitino correctly diagrammed exactly what the Blue Devils would try to do: a long pass to Laettner at the top of the key for a last-second desperation shot. If all had gone well in Pitino's plan, Laettner would have found himself sandwiched between John Pelphrey and Deron Feldhouse, one player in front of him and one behind him. Somehow both players wound up behind Laettner, who swished a 17-foot shot to win the game for Duke.

As Blue Devils fans swarmed the court for a wild celebration, Sean Woods remained flat on his face as if he'd been fatally wounded on the battlefield. He says now, "I just kept hoping I'd wake up and find out it was a bad dream." He might also have been thinking what a terrible time it was for a wrong answer from the ouija board that had predicted Kentucky would beat Duke and advance to the Final Four.

• • •

RICHIE FARMER

Richie Farmer honed his game on a dirt court behind his home in the small eastern Kentucky town of Manchester. It was there that he pretended to be his hero, Kyle Macy, and dreamed of someday wearing the blue and white uniform of the Kentucky Wildcats.

In his junior year of high school, Farmer helped Clay County become the first mountain team in 31 years to win a state championship. He was Kentucky's Mr. Basketball as a senior and earned a scholarship to UK.

Just prior to his first road game with the Wildcats, Richie was informed that all players must travel in a coat and tie. He owned neither. "I had to call my mom and have her go out buy me some stuff," said Richie. "I didn't know anything about neckties."

But Richie Farmer did know plenty about shooting a basketball. On a barnstorming tour of the state following his senior year at Kentucky, Farmer actually made 30 three-point shots in one game at his old high school in Manchester. He scored 110 points that night and insists it wasn't planned that way. "It just sort of happened. I got hot and the guys kept throwing me the ball. I think I got to the 100-point mark with about 15 minutes to go in the game."

That scoring outburst though wasn't as memorable to Richie, as his first conversation with Rick Pitino. "When Coach Pitino got the job, he called me in Manchester to tell me what he expected from me. I read later where he said we talked for 12 minutes and he only understood

Richie Farmer

two minutes of what I said. Well, I only understood about 30 seconds of what he said. Manchester and Manhattan just don't speak the same language."

Gradually their relationship grew into one of mutual respect. "Coach never hassled me about my trademark mustache, which I had first grown as an eighth grader", says Farmer, "but he did go kind of nuts over my hair one time. On a bet, some of the guys, including team captain Reggie Hanson, had hooked me up to get a short haircut with lines shaved in the side, and Coach Pitino really didn't like it Actually he hated it, and he let me know just how much he hated it."

Pitino did admire the fact that Farmer had stayed at Kentucky despite the probation that began in his sophomore year. Richie says, "My parents always instilled in me that once you start something, you never give up. Tough times make you better." The toughest time that year was a 150 to 95 loss at Kansas, which Farmer has never forgotten. "I still can't believe the way Roy Williams of Kansas coached that game. He had his starters out there pressing us when they were up by 40, and they just had so much more talent than we did. We scored 95 points and lost by 55, but from that day on, we started counting down to the rematch. The next year, we beat them by 17, which means we made a 72-point turn around."

In Farmer's senior year, the turnaround in the Kentucky basketball program ended just short of the final four with the gut-wrenching last-second loss to Duke, but Richie says, "Just playing in a game considered maybe the best of all time is something to be very proud of."

• • •

THE UNFORGETTABLES

On the Tuesday night following the Final Four that year, a special night of celebration took place at Rupp Arena to honor a team that had earned the nickname "The Unforgettables." UK athletic director C. M. Newton told the four seniors, Farmer, Feldhaus, Pelphrey, and Woods, "Many have scored more points than you have. They have won more individual honors, but no one can match what you've given us by putting your hearts into the wearing of the Kentucky jersey. Look to the ceiling." When the four looked up, they saw their jerseys hanging from the rafters.

• • •

THE COMEBACK

Just mention the word "comeback" and Kentucky fans automatically think of a February night in 1994 when the Wildcats somehow wiped out a 31-point deficit in 15 frantic minutes at LSU. Coach Dale Brown's LSU Tigers were not having a good season, but on this night, they seemed determined to take out their frustration on Pitino's 11th-ranked Cats.

LSU bombed in nine three-pointers in the first half alone, most of them by freshman sensation Ronnie

Henderson, who had 22 points by intermission. Kentucky trailed by 16 at the break, and reserve guard Chris Harrison recalls, "Coach Pitino still seemed fairly confident at that point. He just made some adjustments and reminded us to never give up."

But things quickly got worse in the second half as LSU scored 18 unanswered points that extended their lead to 31 with 15 minutes left. Harrison says, "At that point, coach called a time-out and just glared at us. He said, 'You guys are gonna pay for this tomorrow in practice.' Then he told me to go in the game, and I remember Travis Ford saying to me, 'You're gonna light it up tonight.' Well, I hit my first shot and the next one, and all of a sudden everybody seemed to get in on the act. We started raining threes just the way they had in the first half."

Harrison, a Kentuckian from the small town of Tollesboro, had once scored 73 points in a high school game, while averaging just under 40 points per contest in his senior year, but his college career had been largely undistinguished to that point. Still, he managed to score eight quick points in a 24-4 run that slashed the Tigers' lead to 11 with just under 10 minutes to go. "We always felt," said Harrison, "that if we were within striking distance at the 10-minute mark, we would probably win because we were in so much better shape than our opponents."

Sure enough, Kentucky just kept chipping away until 6'9" forward Walter McCarty, who hadn't made a single three-point attempt in the previous eight games, swished one to give the Cats a 96-95 lead with 19 seconds to play.

LSU, in a state of shock at that point, failed to score the rest of the way as Kentucky added four free throws and completed one of the most remarkable comebacks ever witnessed in college basketball.

Harrison says, "Looking back on it now, if LSU hadn't taken another shot all night and just started milking the clock after going up by 31, we probably couldn't have scored fast enough to catch them. I'll never forget the look on Dale Brown's face after that game. I think that's probably the night he started considering retirement."

• • •

TRAVIS FORD

NCAA rules prohibit a team from playing in the Maui Classic more than once every four years, but former Wildcat Travis Ford actually played on the winning team in Maui twice. On his first trip to Hawaii as a freshman for the University of Missouri, his Tigers won the tournament, although Ford recalls, "I didn't play great. I just remember it was incredibly hot in that gym in Lahaina." Travis transferred to Kentucky after that season because Missouri was about to be slapped with an NCAA probation, and as a senior with the Wildcats, it was Ford who was incredibly hot in the Maui Classic. He scored 52 points in the Cats' last two games there, including 25 in the finals against a great Arizona team. "I remember that

Travis Ford

as one of the most exciting games I ever played in. I couldn't stop Arizona guard Damon Stoudamire, but he couldn't stop me either. It was some kind of shootout." Ford recalls Coach Rick Pitino being a little more loose than usual in Hawaii. "We were all kind of surprised that he gave us so much free time to walk the beach and enjoys ourselves over there," says Travis. "We thought he might insist that we concentrate on basketball the whole time." These days, Ford can look back and see how much alike he and Coach Pitino were. "We were both really competitive, and I think because of that, we bumped heads quite a bit, but he made me so much better as a player. Coach Pitino was one of the first to really understand the importance of the three-point shot, and he gave us total freedom to shoot it. In fact, after we'd miss a few, he'd encourage us to keep shooting it. His individual instruction in practice also made me a much better shooter. He was a great teacher not just on the mechanics of the jump shot but also on how to get open and how to get the shot off quicker. Being as small as I was growing up, I had always had to go out a little further to get my shots, and so I had practiced a lot from that range." And the practice paid off. In the 1992-93 season, Ford made a school record 101 three-pointers. His almost unbelievable 52.9 percent accuracy from that far out was an SEC record.

• • •

DEREK ANDERSON

In two exhibition games prior to the regular season opener in November of 1995, junior guard Derek Anderson took 16 shots from the field and made 15 of them. His only miss in the exhibition against Athletes in Action was rebounded and put back in by center Mark Pope, who told reporters after the game, "Derek must be having problems with his girlfriend or a test, but we can't have that. It's just unacceptable."

• • •

THE PITINO SHOW

Pitino was notorious for finding something negative to bring up in his postgame comments no matter how well his team had just played, and Kentucky fans had started following the coach's lead. So after an almost flawless 124–80 win over TCU in late January of 1996, Pitino used his radio show to playfully poke fun at himself and the hard-to-please fans. "It's like having a beautiful model in your agency and you're worried about the mole on her arm," he chided. "It's like you're having a great time in life and somebody comes up and says, 'You're gonna die some day.' We want to start enjoying it, live for the moment and worry about the future when it comes." At that point in the season, UK was enjoying 14 consecutive victories.

• • •

CAMERON MILLS

Few players in college basketball have progressed more in four years than Cameron Mills, a 6'3" guard whose father, Terry, played at Kentucky under Adolph Rupp from 1969-71. Recruiters deemed Cameron too slow to compete at a major Division I school, but this so-called slow-poke walked on at UK and wound up earning two NCAA championship rings.

In the summer prior to his freshman year at Kentucky, Mills attended Rick Pitino's camp and got a sudden dose of humility. Pitino told him, "Cameron, you're the fattest [expletive] ballplayer I've ever seen. I can't have you on this team if you're going to look like this." Mills promptly lost 30 pounds over the next three weeks but recalls saying to himself, "I don't know if I can take four years of this man."

In Mills's sophomore year, Pitino decided to field a junior varsity team that practiced every morning at 6 o'clock because that was the only time the court was available. Delray Brooks, the former Providence star, coached the JV squad, and Pitino never showed up for the practice sessions. That was just fine with Cameron Mills, who was grateful for some time away from the "Pitino pressure cooker."

In the very first JV game, Mills scored 38 points against Lee College, but when the team lost for the first time against Hiwassee Junior College, Pitino summoned Cameron to his office along with Nazr Mohammed, Oliver Simmons, and Jason Lathrem and called them "a disgrace to the university." Mills did get to dress for the varsity games, although he got into a game on only seven rare occasions.

He was in his familiar spot at the end of the bench on April 1, 1996, when Kentucky defeated Syracuse for its sixth national championship. When the final buzzer sounded that night, Cameron Mills dropped to his knees, raised his arms to the heavens, and began praising God. Father Ed Bradley, the Wildcats' unofficial team priest, ran over and tried to lift Mills to his feet to give him a celebratory hug. Cameron looks back on that moment with a sense of humor today. "There I was," he says, "trying my best to praise the Lord, and I had a priest telling me to get up and celebrate."

Coach Pitino put Mills on scholarship the next season, but when a reporter asked the coach about Cameron's prospects for more playing time, Pitino replied, "Cameron still can't guard my desk." What Cameron could do, however, was shoot, and when Derek Anderson went down with his knee injury, Pitino needed some offense. Mills recalls, "More than anything right about then, he just needed bodies."

Cameron Mills

On Super Bowl Sunday, the Cats played Arkansas in Fayetteville, and Mills scored a career-high 12 points in 13 minutes, equaling his total playing time for the entire season the year before. Mills scored 16 more in the SEC tournament championship game against Georgia, then made five three-pointers in a 19-point explosion against Montana in the first round of the NCAA tournament.

On the day of the national championship game against Arizona, the Wildcats practiced at a high school gym in Indianapolis. During a brief scrimmage, something happened that Cameron Mills will remember the rest of his life. "Coach Pitino so rarely gave anyone a compliment", says Mills, "that when he did, it was like gold. I remember Wayne Turner got double-teamed and managed to get the ball over to me, and I hit a jump shot. Coach blew his whistle and started screaming at the guy who should have been guarding me. His exact words were, 'You just left the greatest shooter in the country to go and help out on Wayne Turner.' I **spent** the rest of that practice trying not to strut."

After Mills poured in a dozen more points in the heartbreaking loss to Arizona that night, Coach Pitino consoled him in the locker room by saying, "I can't believe what you've accomplished for us, Cameron. I think back to your freshman year when you showed up at a fat 211 pounds. You've got a lot to be proud of, son." Today Cameron Mills says, "I went from hating Coach Pitino to thinking he was the most incredible person on earth."

• • •

Orlin Wagner, AP/Wide World Photos

Tubby Smith

Part Five:

Tubby Smith

Orlando "Tubby" Smith had a tough act to follow at Kentucky. Rick Pitino had taken the Wildcats to the Final Four in consecutive years. On the June day he was introduced as Kentucky's new coach, Tubby told the assembled media, "There's no guarantee that we're gonna be back there at the Final Four this next season, but that's our goal, to be the best team in the country." Fifty years after Adolph Rupp and the Fabulous Five gave Kentucky its first NCAA Championship, Tubby Smith and his "Comeback Cats" did indeed provide the university its seventh national title.

Ask him about his unusual nickname, and Tubby will set the record straight. "I had 16 brothers and sisters, and Saturday night was the only time we got to take a bath. When I got into that tub, I didn't want to get out."

At the hastily called news conference to introduce Smith as Rick Pitino's successor, Tubby was asked if any of the mentors and coaching friends that he called to consult about the Kentucky job had advised him to step back and think more about it before accepting. "No," said Tubby. "In fact, most of 'em said 'If you don't take it, how about recommending me to C. M. Newton?'"

• • •

Tubby Smith and his champion "Comeback Cats"

ALLEN EDWARDS

The youngest of three basketball-playing brothers from Miami, Florida, Allen Edwards had a solid if not spectacular career at Kentucky from 1995 through '98. In mid-January of his senior year, Edwards went into a long slump as he struggled to cope with the knowledge that his mother was losing her battle with breast cancer.

Louisa Mae Edwards died during the SEC tournament in Atlanta. Allen traveled that Friday night with unofficial team chaplain Father Ed Bradley to the family home in Holly Hill, South Carolina. They attended the funeral on Saturday and flew back to Atlanta for the tournament finals against South Carolina on Sunday, but not before Allen received a phone call from his teammates who told him how much they cared about him. Point guard Wayne Turner told him, "We beat Arkansas for you today; now come back and help us beat South Carolina."

Allen Edwards played that SEC tournament final like a man possessed. Replacing the injured Jeff Sheppard at shooting guard, Edwards scored 15 points, handed out five assists, and played ferocious defense on South Carolina star B. J. McKie as the Wildcats trounced the Gamecocks by thirty points.

When Edwards returned to practice on Monday, he noticed that teammate Scott Padgett, who lockered next to him, had written in big bold letters on the sides of his shoes, RIP LME. Allen knew instantly that the letters stood for REST IN PEACE, LOUISA MAE

EDWARDS. He told Padgett, "Thanks, man. I really appreciate that." Looking back on that day, Edwards says, "I remember thinking that a bunch of guys who care that much about one another couldn't help but be successful." After they won the national championship, Allen Edwards called it "the most unselfish team I ever played on."

• • •

REMEMBER THE ALAMODOME

Kentucky trailed Utah by ten points at halftime of the NCAA championship game at the Alamodome in San Antonio. No team had ever come back from a double-digit deficit to win an NCAA title game, but no team in this tournament had had more practice at coming from behind.

The Cats had been down to Stanford in the semifinals, and in the South Regional finals against Duke, they had somehow battled back from a 17-point deficit with only nine and a half minutes to play. Duke scored only three baskets the rest of the way. Time and time again, Kentucky point guard Wayne Turner blew by Steve Wojciechowski to either score or dish off to an open teammate. Cameron Mills's only basket of the NCAA tournament to that point gave the Cats their first lead at 80 to 79, and they hung on to win 86–84.

Wayne Turner played on three NCAA Final Four teams

Pat Forde of Louisville's *The Courier Journal* called Mills "the poster boy for that dream-come-true season. Counted out many times, but an overachieving champion in the end."

Just when it appeared that the Cats were down and out for the last time against Utah, they battled back once more. When Jeff Sheppard came up with a steal and a dazzling dunk that gave Kentucky its first lead of the second half, the players couldn't help but think of all the times Coach Smith had reminded them that "defense wins championships."

• • •

ERIC DANIELS

Tubby Smith has been able to continue the Kentucky tradition of successfully recruiting high school All-Americans, but he has also proven to be adept at finding unpolished gems. Eric Daniels was such a find. Daniels grew an astonishing nine inches during his four years at Princeton High School in Cincinnati.

His freshman year alone, Eric sprouted from 5'10" to 6'2". Midway through his senior season when Kentucky finally began to take notice, Daniels stood 6'7". The growth spurt though took its toll on Eric's knees, and perhaps because the chronic pain kept him from achieving "superstar" status, Daniels was not highly rated by most of the major recruiting services.

Eric Daniels

Even after Kentucky disappointed some of its fans by signing the relatively unheralded Daniels to a scholarship, his knee problems persisted. In fact, the player who had by now earned the nickname "E Diddy" missed several practices and the annual Blue-White scrimmage just prior to his first season as a Wildcat. That just made Eric Daniels's phenomenal college basketball debut all the more astonishing.

Daniels shocked his coaches, teammates, and fans by making 20 of his first 23 shots as a college player, and those shots came from all over the court. Eric now admits that he, too, was amazed as one try after another kept going in.   Of all the great players who have worn Kentucky blue through the years, none ever equaled Daniels's remarkable shooting feat as a raw, first year player.

Eric's unbelievable accuracy kept the Kentucky coaching staff in a constant state of amazement, especially considering his lack of practice time.   In only his second collegiate game, Daniels made practically everything he shot against Jacksonville State and finished with 19 points. Tubby Smith told reporters at the time, "We can't expect him to keep shooting like this forever, but it's sure nice while it lasts."

• • •

RICK'S RETURN...
TUBBY'S MOMENT

When Rick Pitino decided to get back into college coaching after failing to return the Boston Celtics to their past glory, there was no shortage of suitors at his doorstep. The University of Michigan came calling, as did UNLV and others, but the most intriguing offer came from the University of Louisville, just down the road from Lexington. Most Kentucky fans assumed Pitino retained far too much loyalty to the Big Blue to ever seriously consider coaching their biggest in-state rival, and when Rick eventually took the Louisville job, he touched off a firestorm of criticism around the state. Many labeled him a traitor of the highest order.

Using the same pressing, up-tempo style that he had employed to reenergize Kentucky basketball in 1989, Pitino got the Cardinals off to a 9-1 start in his first season at Louisville. Then, on December 29, 2001, he brought his team to Rupp Arena for the annual renewal of the rivalry that had lost some of its former luster in the last years of Denny Crum's reign in Louisville.

One of the largest crowds ever to watch a college basketball game in Kentucky showed up that night, many armed with signs and banners expressing their displeasure with Pitino. One read, "Hey, Louisville, how do you like our hand-me-downs?" But on a night when most folks expected open hostility toward Pitino, the overriding sentiment was unrestrained support for Tubby

Smith. Even louder than the boos when Pitino was introduced was the seemingly endless chant, "Tubby! Tubby!"

Tubby Smith had served as an assistant on Pitino's staff at UK, but he had never beaten his old boss in head-to-head competition. As the hustling Cardinals stayed close to the Cats in the first half, some began to fear that trend would continue, and one can only imagine what the reaction of Kentucky fans might have been if Louisville had indeed won the game, but a fiery halftime speech by Smith seemed to inspire his troops. Kentucky pulled away to win by twenty, and the following morning, the *Lexington Herald-Leader* ran the headline: PITINO'S COME*RUPP*ANCE.

• • •

TAYSHAUN PRINCE

In his junior year at Kentucky, Tayshaun Prince scored what was then a career-high 31 points against Iowa in the second round of the 2001 NCAA tournament. The pencil-thin Prince considered jumping to the NBA after that season but decided to return to Kentucky for his senior year.

It was to be a season full of distractions and controversy and more losses than practically anyone expected, but in the second round of the 2002 NCAA tournament, Prince again dazzled millions of television viewers with a new career-high 41 points against Tulsa.

What made his clutch performance even more remarkable was that it came in St. Louis, Missouri, where Jack Givens had capped off his brilliant UK career with a 41-point performance in the 1978 national championship game against Duke. Tayshaun Prince had not yet been born at the time, but like Givens, Prince was left-handed. Like Givens, Prince wore number 21. Like Givens, Prince saved his highest scoring game as a college player for the NCAA tournament. Tayshaun was aware that Givens was a lefty who once scored 41 points, but when informed afterwards that his own scoring binge had come in the same city that Jack Givens took by storm, the smiling Prince shook his head in amazement and said, "What a coincidence. I guess it's a small world."

Tayshaun also led Kentucky in rebounding, blocked shots, and assists in that game against Tulsa while playing 37 minutes without a single turnover. I asked him if all the fun he had in that game on a national stage validated his decision to stay in school considering all the turmoil of his senior season. His eyes seemed to light up as he replied, "Definitely; I'm glad I stayed for a lot of reasons. First, I think learning to deal with all the distractions we had will really help me in the NBA, but as far as the 41 points are concerned, I'm most proud that I only had to take 21 shots to get them and that I played a good all-around game. The other guys saw how hot I was, and they got me the ball where I could do something with it."

Tayshaun Prince

For a spindly 6'9" forward who looked anything but strong, Prince could do great things long distances from the basket. Earlier in his senior year, Tayshaun had thrilled the Rupp Arena faithful by swishing one long three-point shot after another in a win over North Carolina, but fellow senior J. P. Blevins says that game was very different from the tournament game in St. Louis. "Tayshaun came out against North Carolina and started draining threes right from the start," recalled Blevins, "but against Tulsa, his performance just kept building over the course of the game and the 41 points really kind of snuck up on us." Tayshaun's success as a long-range shooter didn't sneak up on Blevins. "I remember when he first came out to practice as a freshman; right away he started making it look easy to hit the threes no matter how far out he went. I knew right then he was something special."

Even Prince himself had no idea he was having the game of his life in St. Louis. "I knew I was having a really good night," says Tayshaun, "but until I heard the crowd chanting, 'We want 40,' I didn't know I was really that close." Prince made six of eight tries from beyond the three-point arc against Tulsa, including one that beat the buzzer at the end of the first half after the Golden Hurricane had scored 11 straight points to go ahead 42 to 40. He says, "I think I'll be a better shooter in the NBA with the three-point line being further out. I've always felt like I concentrate more the further I am away from the basket."

Prince credits a kinder, gentler Tubby Smith for helping him and several other Wildcats play fearless basketball during the tournament. "After four years of playing for Coach Smith," says Prince, "I was used to his famous stare and getting screamed at sometimes, but some of the guys just couldn't deal with it. I know how much he cares about us and how badly he wants for us to be successful, so I wasn't really surprised that he seemed to have a personality transplant after we played so bad in the SEC tournament. I was just kind of shocked that under all the pressure of the NCAA tournament he would make that drastic change. I think we responded with some of our best basketball of the season."

• • •

C. M. NEWTON

Perhaps no man alive was more closely associated with all five of the Kentucky coaches featured in this book than C. M. Newton. He played under Rupp and later coached against him. He coached against Joe B. Hall and Eddie Sutton, and finally, as UK's athletics director, he hired both Rick Pitino and Tubby Smith.

Only after his 1971 Alabama team beat Kentucky did Newton begin to feel like one of Rupp's peers.

"I was scared of him all the time I played for him," said Newton. "I remember one day when I wasn't playing very well, Coach Rupp pointed me toward the bench and said, 'Go sit down, you remind me of a Shetland pony in a stud horse parade.'"

Years later, even when Newton's talented Alabama teams performed well against Rupp's Kentucky teams, C. M. remembers any postgame praise came with a caveat. "Coach Rupp would say things like, 'You had your team well prepared tonight, but I'm afraid you're going to have to simplify your offense.'"

Newton says Joe B. Hall never received the accolades he deserved for his coaching at Kentucky.

"I tried to convince Joe to become part of my Alabama staff before it became evident that he would succeed Adolph at Kentucky," says C. M. "Every game against Joe's teams you just knew you were gonna be in a war because he had them so well prepared. We went with a small lineup against his twin towers of Robey and Phillips one night in Tuscaloosa," recalls Newton. "We put 6'6" Regggie King in the post, but Joe just matched smaller guys with smaller guys. It was hard to outsmart him."

Newton was hired as director of athletics at Kentucky on April 1, 1989, following perhaps the most disappointing year in the long and storied history of UK basketball. Eddie Sutton's final season had resulted in a 13-19 record. C. M. says, "Eddie should not be remembered for that one bad year, and I'm sure he won't be. The man could flat coach. I always loved watching his teams play, but there were just too many negative things swirling around for him to be successful that last year here." Newton's daunting task was to find just the right coach to rebuild the program and to recapture the glory of the past. Just as importantly, he knew he must find a coach good enough to do it while running a squeaky clean program free of any NCAA violations.

His short list of candidates included former UK star Pat Riley, who had gone on to great success as a coach in the NBA. Riley wasn't ready to make a move at the time, and talks with highly regarded college coaches like Lute Olsen, Mike Krzyzewski, and P. J. Carlisemo merely resulted in all three staying where they were.

Newton's ace in the hole was Rick Pitino, who was involved at the time in trying to get his New York Knicks into the NBA playoffs. "I knew that Rick could coach a team to be champions rather than just recruit a championship team," said Newton. "And I also knew his style of play would put the fun back into Kentucky basketball. He was one of the very first coaches to grasp the possibilities of the three-point shot."

Newton's favorite story about his relationship with Pitino centers around the famous 1992 game with Duke in the Mideast Regional finals. C. M. remembers, "Rick was absolutely devastated following Christian Laettner's game winning shot. I got to him as quickly as I could and told him that the loss might actually be a blessing in disguise. I pointed out that he had worked miracles with this particular Kentucky team, which didn't really possess Final Four talent. I told him that it's possible to accomplish too much too soon, and by doing that you create unrealistic expectations. Rick looked at me like I had gone absolutely crazy."

Pitino was a purist with great respect for basketball traditions, both college and professional, and when he accepted the challenge of restoring the Boston Celtics franchise to its former glory, C. M. Newton had to again go looking for the right man to coach the Kentucky Wildcats. This time he started with an even shorter list of candidates.

Newton says, "I had recommended Tubby Smith to Rick Pitino as an assistant coach. When Tubby became a head coach first at Tulsa and later at Georgia, I watched him win quickly with other people's players. I remember telling Georgia athletic director Vince Dooley that if Rick ever left Kentucky, I would come after Tubby Smith."

Newton knew that selecting an African American to lead the basketball program would not be a unanimously popular decision with UK fans across the state, but he was totally convinced it was the right decision. C. M. had integrated the basketball program as coach at the University of Alabama. At a time when other SEC schools were cautiously breaking the color barrier, Newton was starting five black players simply because, as he says, "They were my five best players."

"I never set out to integrate anything," says C. M. "I just don't see things in terms of color. My high school basketball coach in Ft. Lauderdale, Florida, had come from Mississippi where attempts at integration had been slow to evolve, but he was completely color-blind. He treated everyone he came in contact with exactly the same, and I think I learned from him to base my evaluations of people on merit regardless of race or ethnic background."

Newton now says, "I was absolutely certain when I hired Tubby Smith that he would be very successful at Kentucky, but I felt exactly the same way when I hired Bill Curry as our football coach, and unfortunately I eventually had to fire Bill."

• • •

SUPERFAN

The fanaticism of Kentucky rooters is legendary. The Wildcats have had some unbelievably avid fans through the years, but perhaps none more faithful than Bob Wiggins. The retired highway engineer for the Kentucky Department of Transportation has attended more than 1,200 games since seeing his first one in 1944. At one point, Wiggins witnessed 615 straight games in person.

Only a heart attack stopped his streak. Wiggins was scheduled to accompany the Cats on their trip to the Great Alaska Shootout on a November morning in 1996, "but," he says, "The pain in my chest was so bad when I woke up that morning, I knew I'd have to let them go without me." Bob Wiggins spent a week in the hospital, all the while pestering his doctors to grant him an early release.

He did manage to watch all the games from Alaska on television, and prior to the first one, he actually placed a call to the courtside table of his friend Ralph Hacker, the play-by-play announcer on the UK Radio Network. Hacker was talking with Wildcats guard Jeff Sheppard when the phone rang. Wiggins recalls, "Ralph told me he had someone there who wanted to speak to me. He handed the phone to Jeff, and several people have related to me since then that Sheppard looked up at the clock before saying to me, 'You've still got time to make it here if you hurry.'"

Wiggins's streak began with a ten-hour drive to Lawrence, Kansas, in 1977. Ironically, his traveling companion that day was Steve Rardin, who would later have his own consecutive game streak of 627 snapped by a heart attack while attending a road game at Syracuse in 1986.

When asked if his employers ever objected to his time on the road with the Cats, Wiggins replied, "No, I saved up my vacation days, and after almost every road game, I would head home immediately, sometimes driving all night and going to work the next morning with no sleep."

Wiggins admits he has no other hobbies besides Kentucky basketball. "I don't play golf, I don't hunt," he says. "After the last game each season, I sit down and start waiting for the next season to begin."

• • •

RAJON RONDO

Rajon Rondo has become one of the greatest professional basketball players ever to play their college ball at the University of Kentucky.

But many don't know that Rondo's first sport wasn't basketball—it was soccer.

"I grew up playing soccer," the star Boston Celtics point guard said. "I was always kicking a ball around."

Luckily for Kentucky and the Celtics, Rondo did pick up a basketball, and using his huge hands, became a local legend at Eastern High in Louisville before moving on to legendary hoops school Oak Hill Academy in Virginia.

But then Rondo had another decision to make. Many thought Rondo would return home and play for Rick Pitino's Louisville squad. But Pitino never really showed Rondo the love; instead, Pitino was recruiting national point guard darling Sebastian Telfair out of New York. While that was going on, Tubby Smith, then the coach at rival Kentucky, offered Rondo a scholarship.

Looking back, Pitino never had a chance. Derek Anderson, who was also from Louisville and played for Pitino at UK, says Rondo would have never played for the Louisville coach. Anderson's son was best friends with Rondo, and when Rondo asked the former UK star what it was like to play for Pitino, Anderson was honest.

"Coach Pitino is a yeller," Anderson said. "And yelling doesn't work with Rajon. They would have never gotten along. Tubby is much more Rajon's style."

And that's how it worked. Rondo went to UK, played two seasons (beating Louisville twice), led a team to the Elite Eight, and became an All-Star pro, winning a World Championship with the Celtics.

As for Telfair? He never played at Louisville, deciding instead to jump straight to the NBA, where he does not start. Pitino got neither guard. Later on, he called not pursuing Rondo his greatest recruiting mistake.

But it doesn't matter. Pitino never really had a chance anyway.

• • •

Part Six:

Billy Gillispie

After a decade of wins and pressure, Tubby Smith decided in 2007 to leave UK for Minnesota. His replacement didn't fare too well.

In all honesty, the short, two-year reign of Billy Gillispie was a disaster. There was a loss to Gardner Webb. And another to Virginia Military Institute. And another to San Diego.

And those were all at home. In the first season, the Wildcats barely made the NCAA Tournament. In the second, they missed it and settled for the NIT. As the losses piled up, the tension grew. Gillispie was rude to reporters and, some said, to former and current players. Some said he forced players to play injured. Some said he drank and socialized too much. Some said his disciplinary tactics (forcing players to sit in a bathroom stall at halftime) bordered on insanity.

It was all too bizarre. Whether it was getting short with UK play-by-play man Tom Leach on a daily basis or running from local sportscaster Alan Cutler as Gillispie tried to elude reporters the day he was fired, nothing about Gillispie's tenure seemed normal.

The coach from Texas seemed to loathe the spotlight required of being the head man at Kentucky. But he could be charming on a one-on-one basis, and frequently he was known to give thousands of dollars to local charities. If Gillispie heard of a UK fan suffering from cancer, he would reach out to that person. If someone had a dream to go to Rupp Arena, he would make it happen.

But he was not the right man for the UK job.

"Coach Gillispie is a very smart coach," former UK player Josh Harrellson told ASeaofBlue.com after the coach left. "He knew basketball. I don't think he had the best way of teaching it. But I'm very thankful for what he did. He made all of us mentally tough."

• • •

JODIE MEEKS

Jodie Meeks stood at the line and took a deep breath.

Locked in a tighter-than-one-would-like game with archival Tennessee in Knoxville, Meeks had done all he could by himself, scoring 48 points, and he was ready to add two more to crack the magical half-century mark. Never one to talk much during games, the star guard from Norcross, Ga. couldn't help but celebrate as his free throws went through the hoop.

"Forty-nine," he chirped.

And as the second free throw went in:

"Fiddy," he said.

Meeks had been having an interesting season—not what he'd envisioned when he fell in love with UK and Tubby Smith nearly four years prior.

Since then, Tubby left, Billy Gillispie had been hired, and the new coach and his star player had failed to see exactly eye to eye. Gillispie questioned his toughness and openly wondered if Meeks took too many shots.

On Jan. 13, 2009, Meeks had a night athletes dream about. Up only four points at the half, Kentucky needed most of Meeks' career scoring mark, which resulted in a UK record,for a total of 54 points. Kentucky won 90-72.

Meeks hit 10 three-pointers and all 14 of his free throws on the night. His 54 points broke Dan Issel's 39-year single game scoring record of 53, which set against Ole Miss.

"It means a lot to be in the same sentence as Dan Issel," Meeks told ESPN. "It's mind-boggling. I was just out there playing to win."

• • •

THE TORNADO GAME

Originally scheduled to be played at the Georgia Dome, the 2008 SEC Tournament got derailed by Mother Nature.

Night had fallen by the end of the third game between Mississippi State and Alabama on March 14.
The two teams were battling into overtime, but outside,
storms were brewing. The National Weather Service
had issued a tornado warning at 9:26 p.m., and at 9:40
p.m. a tornado hit downtown Atlanta and the Georgia
Dome. The storm tore open a panel on the north side of
the dome, and bolts and insulation fell into the arena.

By 10:30, the storm had passed and the teams came
back on to the court to finish the game. SEC officials
decided not to play the fourth game between Kentucky
and Georgia, and instead, they postponed it until early
the next morning at Georgia Tech. We all know how
Kentucky fans travel, but due to the smaller venue, only
officials, media, 400 fans and players' families were allowed into the game, negating what would have been an
overwhelming UK fan advantage.

So, an underachieving UK squad (still 12-4 in the
SEC) lost to Georgia, a team that finished 4-12 in the
conference with a sub-.500 record overall, by a score of
60-56 in overtime. Amazingly, Georgia went on to win
two more games (for a total of three wins in 30 hours) to
take their first tourney crown since 1983.

Kentucky's season ended prematurely. But now we
know: You can't beat Mother Nature.

• • •

JEANNINE EDWARDS

The question seemed innocent enough. After Ole Miss had held Jodie Meeks to six points during the first half of a 2009 contest, ESPN sideline reporter Jeannine Edwards asked then-Kentucky Head Coach Billy Gillispie what the Rebels had done to contain the Wildcats' leading scorer.

"This is Kentucky, it's not Jodie Meeks," Gillispie replied in a snarky manner, smiling the whole time. "This is not a one-man team. That's really a bad question."

Edwards, who was much more professional in the situation, responded with another query.

"What adjustments have you made on defense since the beginning of the first half?" she asked. Gillispie responded with a much more refined answer, as he complimented the Rebels before going into the locker room.

Gillispie's behavior was an embarrassment and was a harbinger of what would happen in a few short months: Gillispie was fired.

Later the next season, Edwards appeared on new Kentucky Coach John Calipari's "Hot Seat" show, where she good naturedly lampooned the Gillispie situation.

Calipari asked Edwards how tough it was to thrive in a male-dominated sport.

"Cal, that is a stupid question," she said, laughing.

PART SEVEN:

John Calipari

Undefeated. Forty wins, zero losses. That's the goal.

That's what John Calipari said after he won a national title with the Kentucky Wildcats in 2012, with a record of 38-2. And that's why UK fans love him—because he is just as crazy as they are. Calipari was hired in 2009 to clean up the mess Billy Gillispie had made. While there were some talented players in the program (Darius Miller and Patrick Patterson), Calipari brought in the first of five consecutive No. 1-ranked recruiting classes, led by John Wall, DeMarcus Cousins, and Eric Bledsoe.

That first team was a juggernaut, and in landing Wall, it became once again cool to go to Kentucky. And Calipari (unlike Gillispie) understood the role of being the Kentucky coach. He encouraged former players to come back for reunions and to serve on the coaching staff to earn their degrees; he became a leader in college sports on social media sites like Facebook and Twitter; he developed inroads to China with coaches and players; he organized a benefit for earthquake relief in Haiti that raised more than $1 million; he preached a "Players First" mentality in the program, which became the calling card for every talented player who wanted to star in the NBA; and most of all, Calipari won a lot (he did not lose a game at home until his third season).

For UK, it was a match made in Heaven. On Dec. 21, 2009, Kentucky became the first program to reach 2,000 wins with an 88-44 victory over Drexel, and ESPN aired the celebration live after the game. Rupp Arena became the place to be. Celebrities like Lebron James, Magic Johnson, the rapper Drake, and filmmaker Spike Lee attended UK games.

But the coronation came in 2012, when Calipari's team brought home the school's eighth national championship. To celebrate, the coach got on a bus and escorted the trophy all around the state so fans could see it.

Crazy. Just like the Big Blue Nation.

• • •

DEMARCUS COUSINS

Call me!

Long before a Canadian starlet sang out the words "Call Me Maybe," UK's DeMarcus Cousins had a "Call Me" hit of his own.

Big Cuz, as he was known, had developed a reputation as a tough, physical—and sometimes borderline unstable—player, one whose skin opposing fans thought they could get under if they heckled him during a game. In February of 2010 Kentucky was on a roll, losing just one game and earning a No. 2 national ranking. Going into a week where the Cats would play Mississippi State in Starkville, somehow a group of erstwhile Bulldog students obtained Cousins' phone number.

They called him all day and night leading up to the game. Eventually, Cousins had to turn off the phone.

But Cuz got those fans back—to the tune of 19 points, 14 rebounds, and an 81-75 overtime victory. On one play, Cousins snatched an offensive rebound away from a State player, then slammed a dunk back over the top of the Bulldog. The rowdy crowd got very quiet.

Cousins added insult to injury when he then looked up into the student section, mimicked holding a phone to his ear, and yelled "Call me!" to the crowd.

Cuz, whom ESPN's Brad Nessler likened to "a tree planted in the middle of your driveway," went on to become an All-American. Now he has someone else take all his calls.

• • •

BRANDON KNIGHT

Before Brandon Knight etched his name into the UK record books, before he hit game-winning shots against

Ohio State and Princeton in the 2011 NCAA Tournament, before he poured in three after three against West Virginia and North Carolina on the way to the Final Four, the UK point guard was doubted by fans.

Could he do the job? Could he do it the way Coach John Calipari's former point guards had? Like Derrick Rose and John Wall had?

Turns out, he could. But it took his team a while to come around. Almost a whole season, in fact.

When Kentucky faced Florida on Feb. 26, 2011 in Rupp Arena, the Wildcats really needed to win to ensure their place in the NCAA Tournament. They were 7-6 in the SEC and in danger of falling out of the Top 25. Those who were there the day before, including ESPN's Jimmy Dykes, say UK had its best practice all year.

It translated to the court, as UK beat No. 13 Florida 76-68, and Brandon Knight said it was that win that got the Wildcats rolling. In fact, they did not lose again until they were in the Final Four—10 straight wins, including an SEC Tournament title, another win over Florida, and a victory over then-No. 1 Ohio State.

"They [Florida] were the top team in the conference and we were able to beat them," Knight said. "We really started to trust each other, we really pulled together as a team to go into battle."

Knight led the way, before leaving after that freshman season, just as Rose and Wall had done. He averaged 17 points per game in one of the greatest seasons a UK freshman had ever had.

Later that summer, Knight fulfilled a childhood dream when he was the eighth pick in the NBA Draft, selected by the Detroit Pistons.

• • •

JOSH HARRELLSON

It began when Josh Harrellson came to UK's campus in 2008. He was wearing cutoff jean shorts. A popular fan website nicknamed him "Jorts," and the nickname stuck.

Under Coach Billy Gillispie, Harrellson did not fare well, and incoming coach John Calipari kept him because of his outside shooting ability. That said, not much was thought of the junior college transfer from St. Charles, Mo. Certainly no one thought the 6-10, 275-pound big man would make a difference in his UK career, not to mention lead a team to the Final Four.

But he did. And all it took was some, um, motivation. In his senior season, Harrellson was slated to back up incoming freshman center Enes Kanter, from Turkey. But because he played professionally overseas, Kanter was ruled ineligible by the NCAA. Harrellson would have to start.

In the annual preseason Blue/White scrimmage, Harrellson played his best, grabbing 26 rebounds, but Calipari was less than impressed afterward and said so. Harrellson responded via Twitter: "Just amazing to me I can't get a good job or way to go ... It is just amazing to me but I look past it and keep trucking!"

The next day Harrellson had his Twitter privileges revoked, and he was made to run the gymnasium steps early each morning. The result was that he got in the best shape of his life, and every day he worked against Kanter in practice. Slowly, Harrellson developed into a great college center. At Louisville, he earned Player of the Game honors, dropping 23 points and 14 rebounds in a win over the rivals. In the NCAA Tourney, he led the team to the Final Four, with this statline along the way against All-American Jared Sullinger: 17 points, 10 rebounds, and three blocks.

It was an incredible performance to top off an incredible senior year. After the season, Harrellson was selected in the second round of the NBA Draft by the New York Knicks.

It's pretty accurate to say Jorts owed a lot to that one little Tweet.

• • •

ANTHONY DAVIS

As the seconds ran down on the legendary victory, the crowd cheered (especially those clad in blue), and

Anthony Davis, the 6-foot-10 point guard in a center's body for UK, shouted to the fans:

"This is MY state! My state!"

It was out of character for Davis, the freshman All-American and Kentucky's only Player of the Year, who rarely showed any emotion on or off the court.

But the Kentucky and Louisville rivalry can do that to you. Especially when the two teams meet for the first time in the Final Four. It happened in the 2012 NCAA Tournament. Kentucky looked to be the best team in the country, ranked No. 1 and steamrolling to a national title. But in their way stood the upstart Cards.

Kentucky (then ranked No. 3) had defeated No. 4 Louisville 69-62 earlier that year in Lexington. For the second installment, both teams were better. But UofL had no match for Davis, who filled his stat line like this: 18 points, 14 rebounds, two assists, one steal, and five blocked shots in a nearly identical 69-61 UK win. It was a game, and a performance, for the ages. Kentucky would go on to win the school's eighth national title, and Davis became the No. 1 overall pick in the NBA Draft.

His state, indeed.

• • •

DARIUS MILLER

Darius Miller lived the dream. After helping the Wildcats win the national championship in 2012, Miller was drafted in the second round of the NBA Draft and made the New Orleans Hornets team. But before that, he was a high schooler for Mason County in Maysville, Ky.

As a senior in high school, Miller won a state championship, leading his team to victory on the Rupp Arena floor. After that he was named Mr. Basketball.

Then he signed with Kentucky, and as a senior, he won that national title. He is the only UK player to be Mr. Basketball, win a state title, and also win a national championship.

Proving that for some, basketball dreams really do come true.

• • •

NERLENS NOEL

As Kentucky fans, we had been here before: Waiting, hoping, our eyes glued to a TV set as a 17- or 18-year-old kid makes his decision on where he will attend college. Nowadays, most talented high school basketball players make their decisions live on ESPN U by picking up a ball cap signifying their choice.

Not Nerlens Noel.

Nerlens, rated the best center in high school in America, was trying to decide between Kentucky, Syracuse, and Georgetown. The Massachusetts native, who wears a signature high-top fade haircut, decided to have his school's logo cut into the back of his head, which he then covered up with a hoodie so no one could see.

When it came time to announce his decision on TV in the spring of 2012, Noel simply took off the hoodie and turned around to reveal a perfectly cut UK logo.

Once again, the No. 1 recruit was going to Kentucky.

BIBLIOGRAPHY

Farmer, Richie. (1992) *Richie.* Antex Corporation.

Lancaster, Harry & Ledford, Cawood. (1979) *Adolph Rupp As I Knew Him.* Lexington Productions, Inc.

Ledford, Cawood. (1997) *Six Roads to Glory.* Host Communications, Inc.

McKenzie, Michael. (1996) *Oklahoma State University History—Making Basketball.* Walsworth Publishing Company.

Mills, Cameron & Downing, Brooks. (1998) *A Dream Come True.* Addax Publishing Group.

Nelli, Bert & Nelli, Steve. (1998) *The Winning Tradition: A History of Kentucky Wildcat Basketball.* The University Press of Kentucky.

Pitino, Rick & Weiss, Dick. (1992) *Full-Court Pressure.* Hyperion.

Rice, Russell. (1994) *Adolph Rupp: Kentucky's Basketball Baron.* Sagamore Publishing.

Rice, Russell. (1987) *Big Blue Machine.* Strode Publishers.

Ross, Alan. (1999) *Wildcat Wisdom.* Walnut Grove Press.

Vaught, Jamie H. (1999) *Cats Up Close.* McClanahan Publishing House.